CAPITOL REEF
NATIONAL PARK
ACTIVITY BOOK

PUZZLES, MAZES, GAMES, AND MORE ABOUT
CAPITOL REEF NATIONAL PARK

NATIONAL PARKS ACTIVITIES SERIES

CAPITOL REEF NATIONAL PARK ACTIVITY BOOK

Copyright 2021
Published by Little Bison Press

The author acknowledges that the land on which Capitol Reef National Park is located are the traditional lands of Ute and Southern Paiute Tribes.

LITTLE BISON
Press

For more free national parks activities, visit
Littlebisonpress.com

About Capitol Reef National Park

Capitol Reef National Park is located in the desert in the state of Utah. The park's name is for two parts: the word "capitol" is for the white domes of Navajo Sandstone that look similar to some capitol building domes. The second half of the name, "reef" is for the rocky cliffs which are difficult to travel over, like a reef in the ocean.

This park is famous for the Waterpocket Fold, a nearly 100-mile long wrinkle in the Earth's crust. This geologic formation was shaped by deposition, uplift, and erosion. It is the longest exposed monocline, a one-sided fold, on the North American Continent. It is unique as you are able to see 19 different layers of rocks!

Visitors can go to Fruita, a settlement in the desert. This town was home to Mormon pioneers who worked the land and planted fruit orchards that can still be seen today.

Capitol Reef National Park is **famous for:**
- Fremont Culture Petroglyphs
- The Waterpocket Fold
- Mormon pioneers

Hey! I'm Parker!

I'm the only snail in history to visit every National Park in the United States! Come join me on my adventures in Capitol Reef National Park.

Throughout this book, we will learn about the history of the park, the animals and plants that live here, and things to do here if you ever get to visit in person. This book is also full of games and activities!

Last but not least, I am hidden 9 times on different pages. See how many times you can find me. This page doesn't count!

Capitol Reef Bingo

Let's play bingo! Cross off each box that you are able to during your visit to the national park. Try to get a bingo down, across, or diagonally. If you can't visit the park, use the bingo board to plan your perfect trip.

Pick out some activities that you would want to do during your visit. What would you do first? How long would you spend there? What animals would you try to see?

DRINK EXTRA WATER	SEE HOODOOS	IDENTIFY A TREE	TAKE A PICTURE AT AN OVERLOOK	WATCH A MOVIE AT THE VISITORS CENTER
GO FOR A HIKE	LEARN ABOUT THE INDIGENOUS PEOPLE THAT LIVE IN THIS AREA	WITNESS A SUNRISE OR SUNSET	OBSERVE THE NIGHT SKIES	GO STARGAZING
HEAR A BIRD CALL	EAT A PIECE OF FRUIT OR FRUIT PIE	FREE SPACE	WALK THROUGH A FRUIT ORCHARD	VISIT A RANGER STATION
PICK UP TEN PIECES OF TRASH	GO CAMPING	SEE A DESERT BIGHORN SHEEP	VISIT THE GIFFORD HOMESTEAD	SPOT A BIRD OF PREY
LEARN ABOUT THE WATERPOCKET FOLD	SEE SOMEONE ROCK CLIMBING	HAVE A PICNIC	SPOT SOME ANIMAL TRACKS	PARTICIPATE IN A RANGER-LED ACTIVITY

The National Park Logo

The National Park System has over 400 units in the US. Just like Capitol Reef National Park, each location is unique or special in some way. The areas include other national parks, historic sites, monuments, seashores, and other recreation areas.

Each element of the National Park emblem represents something that the National Park Service protects. Fill in each blank below to show what each symbol represents.

```
WORD BANK:
_____

MOUNTAINS, ARROWHEAD, BISON,
SEQUOIA TREE, WATER
```

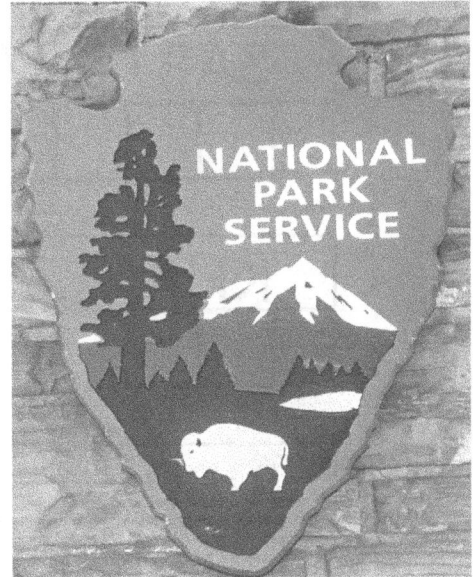

This represents all plants. _____

This represents all animals. _____

This symbol represents the landscapes. _____

This represents the waters protected by the park service. _____

This represents the historical and archeological values. _____

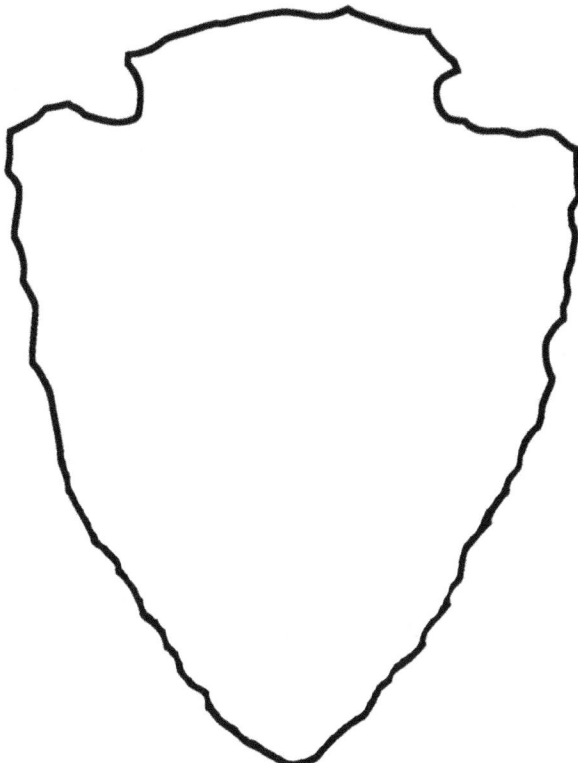

Now it's your turn! Pretend you are designing a new national park. Add elements to the design that represent the things that your park protects

What is the name of your park?

Describe why you included the symbols that you included. What do they mean?

Things to Do Jumble

Unscramble the letters to uncover activities you can do while in Capitol Reef National Park. Hint: each one ends in -ing.

1. SARTGZA [ ][ ][ ][ ][ ][ ][ ] ING

Word Bank

birding
reading
camping
stargazing
horseback riding
hiking
hunting
singing
yelling
sightseeing
picnicking

2. KHI [ ][ ][ ] ING

3. RIBD [ ][ ][ ][ ] ING

4. MAPC [ ][ ][ ][ ] ING

5. KINICPC [ ][ ][ ][ ][ ][ ][ ] ING

6. ESSTEIGH [ ][ ][ ][ ][ ][ ][ ][ ] ING

7. RABEHOSRCKID [ ][ ][ ][ ][ ][ ][ ][ ][ ][ ][ ][ ][ ][ ] ING

Color the Golden Throne

The Golden Throne is a 7,041-foot mountain in Capitol Reef National Park.

Go Birdwatching at Fruita

start here

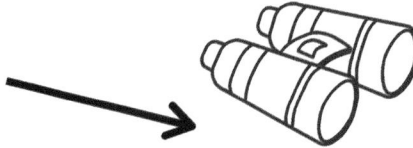

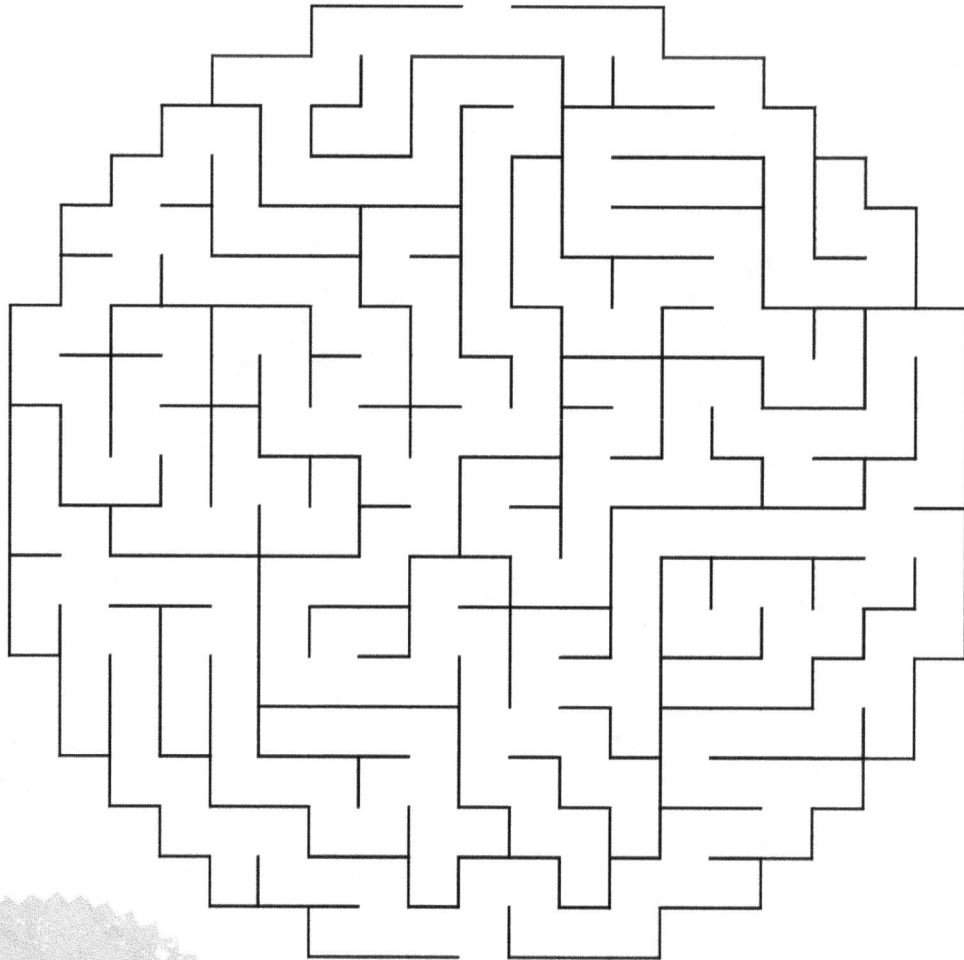

DID YOU KNOW?
Capitol Reef National Park is home to several birds of prey, including eagles, hawks, and owls. Birds of prey are birds that hunt other animals for food.

Exploring the Dark Sky

This park is a popular destination for stargazing. You may see stars in the night sky here that you may not see at home. Why do you think that is?

For all of time, people from across the world have looked at the night sky and seen images in the stars. They created stories about groups of stars, also called constellations. Create your own constellation that you see in the starfield below!

What is your constellation named?

Capitol Reef National Park

Date: _____

Season: _____

Who I went with: _____

Which entrance: _____

How was your experience? Write a few sentences on your trip. Where did you stay? What did you do? What was your favorite activity? If you have not yet visited the park, write a paragraph pretending that you did.

_____

_____

_____

_____

_____

_____

STAMPS

Many national parks and monuments have cancellation stamps for visitors to use. These rubber stamps record the date and the location that you visited. Many people collect the markings as a free souvenir. Check with a ranger to see where you can find a stamp during your visit. If you aren't able to find one, you can draw your own.

Where is the Park?

Capitol Reef National Park is in the northwest United States. It is located in Utah. The nickname for Utah is the Beehive State. Can you find Utah on the map?

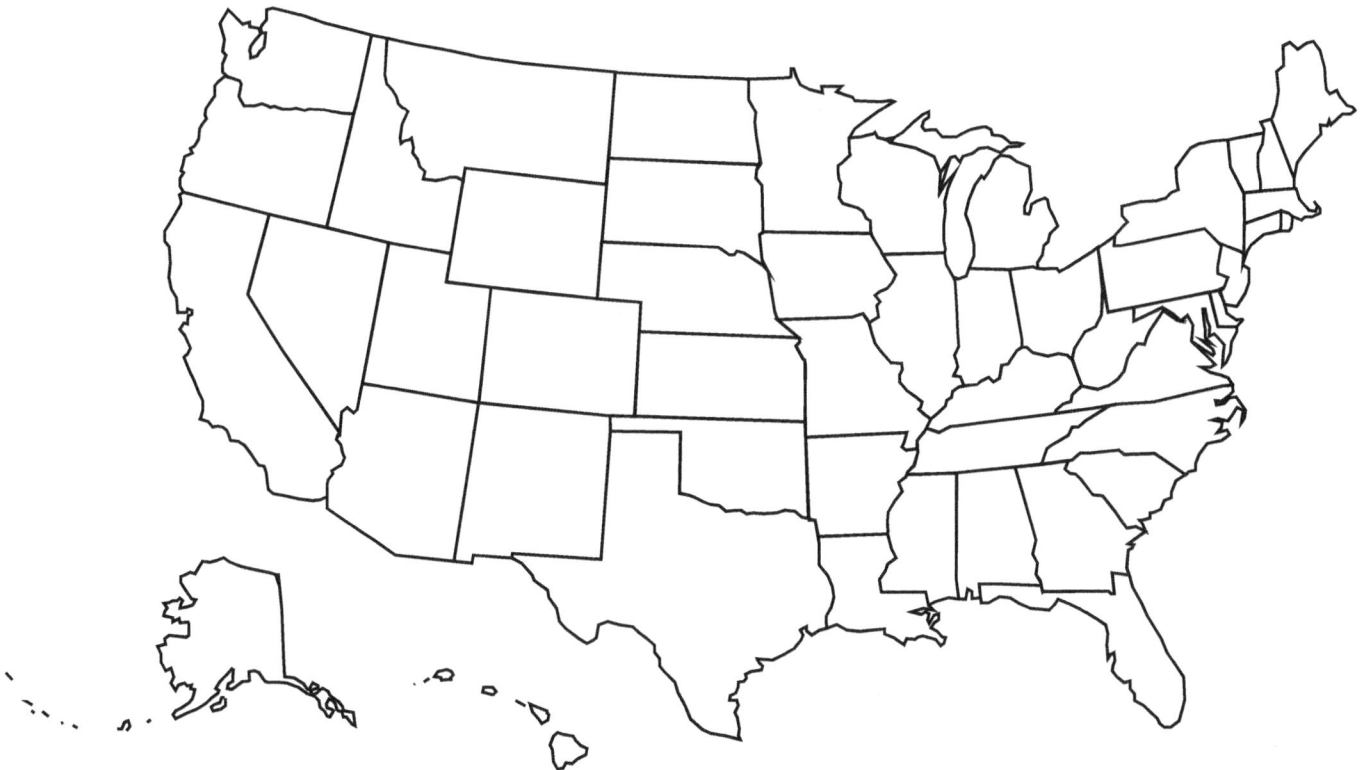

Utah

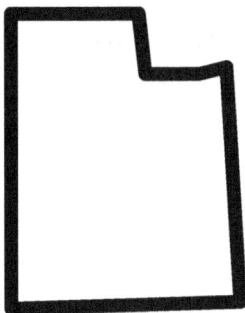

Look at the shape of Utah. Can you find it on the map? If you are from the US, can you find your home state? Color Utah red. Put a star on the map where you live. Color the rest of the map any way you want.

Connect the Dots #1

Connect the dots to figure out what this tiny critter is. There are three or four types of these that live in Capitol Reef National Park.

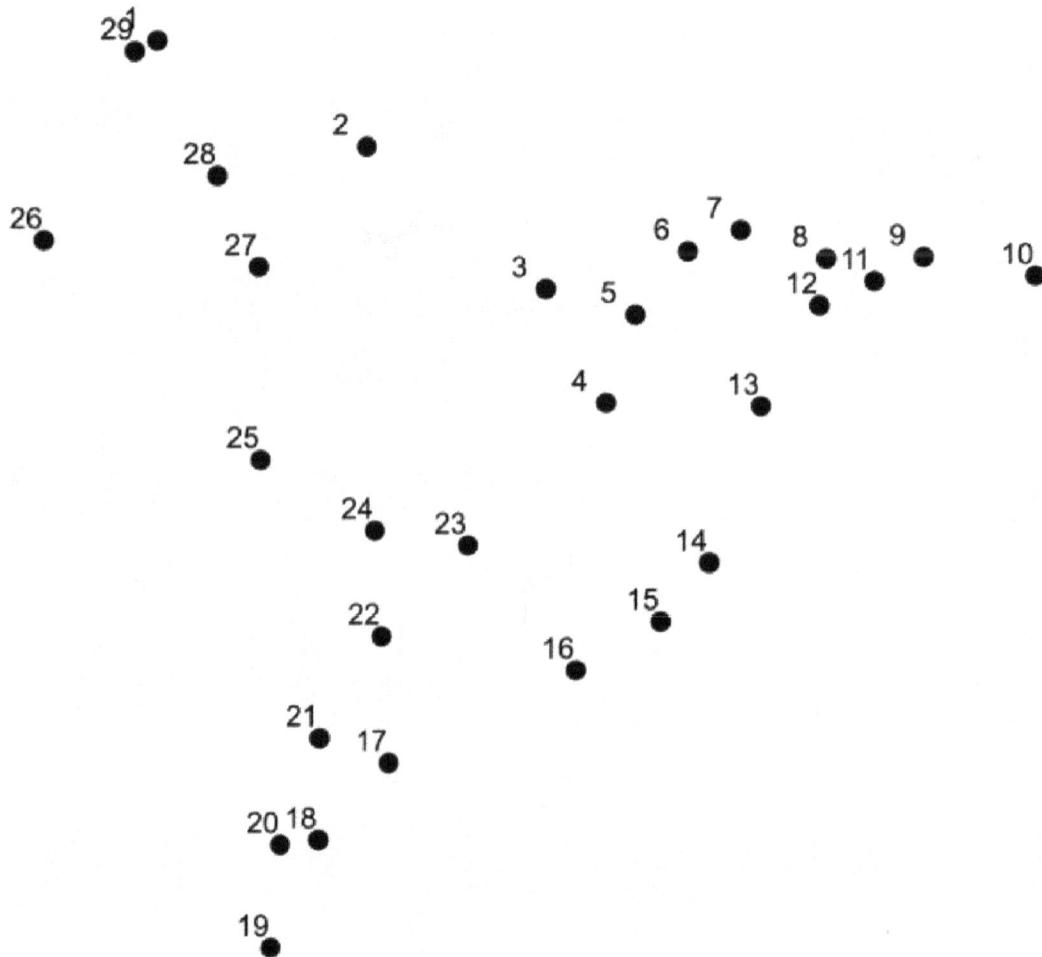

1
29
2
28
26
7
27
6
3   5   8   11   9   10
12
4   13
25
24   23
14
15
22
16
21   17
20 18
19

Their heart rate can reach as high as 1,260 beats per minute and a breathing rate of 250 breaths per minute. Have you ever measured your breathing rate? Ask a friend or family member to set a timer for 60 seconds. Once they say "go", try to breathe normally. Count each breath until they say "stop." How do your breaths per minute compare to hummingbirds?

_____

_____

Whiptail lizards are relatively small lizards with long tails. There are two species of whiptails that live in Capitol Reef National Park.

Ringtails are members of the raccoon family. They have been seen in the Fruita and Pleasant Creek areas of Capitol Reef. However, these agile animals are nocturnal so they are hard to spot during the daytime.

Who Lives in Capitol Reef?

Here are some plants and animals that live in the park. Use the word bank to fill in the clues below. Pay attention to how many letters each word has to see where it fits.

S

O

U

T

H

W

E

S

T

WORD BANK:

CHEATGRASS, GOPHER SNAKE, BOBCAT, CANYON WREN, MULE DEER, PRICKLY PEAR, COTTONTAIL, OSPREY, WHIPTAIL

Bighorn sheep are named for the large horns grown by the males of the species. In Capitol Reef, they can often be seen in areas south of Fruita.

The canyon wren is found in Capitol Reef in places near the canyons and cliffs. Its long curved beak and flat head allow this bird to find insects and spiders deep in rocky crevices.

Common Names
vs.
Scientific Names

A common name of an organism is a name that is based on everyday language. You have heard the common names of plants, animals, and other living things on tv, in books, and at school. Common names can also be referred to as "English" names, popular names, or farmer's name. Common names can vary from place to place. The word for a particular tree may be one thing, but that same tree has a different name in another country. Common names can even vary from region to region, even in the same country.

Scientific names, or Latin names, are given to organisms to make it possible to have uniform names for the same species. Scientific names are in Latin. You may have heard plants or animals referred to by their scientific name, or at least parts of their scientific names. Latin names are also called "binomial nomenclature" which refers to a two-part naming system. The first part of the name - the generic name -names the genus to which the species belongs. The second part of the name, the specific name, identifies the species. For example, Tyrannosaurus rex is an example of a widely known scientific name.

American Black Bear

Ursus americanus

COMMON NAME

Bighorn Sheep

Ovis canadensis

LATIN NAME = GENUS + SPECIES

Bighorn Sheep = Ovis canadensis

Black Bear = Ursus americanus

Find the Match!
Common Names and Latin Names

Match the common name to the scientific name for each animal. The first one is done for you. Use clues on the page before and after this one to complete the matches.

Bighorn Sheep	Haliaeetus leucocephalus
Two-needle Piñon	Ursus americanus
Cheatgrass	Pandion haliaetus
American Black Bear	Opuntia engelmannii
Great Horned Owl	Pinus edulis
Bald Eagle	Aspidoscelis uniparens
Osprey	Bubo virginianus
Prickly Pear	Ovis canadensis
Whiptail	Bromus tectorum

(Cheatgrass is connected by a line to Bromus tectorum)

Bald Eagle

Haliaeetus leucocephalus

Osprey
Pandion haliaetus

Two-needle Piñon
Pinus edulis

Great Horned Owl
Bubo virginianus

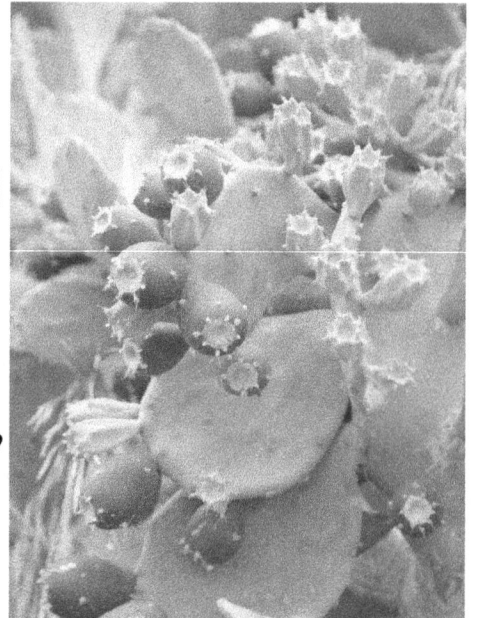

Some plants and animals that live in Utah

Prickly Pear
Opuntia engelmannii

Cheatgrass
Bromus tectorum

Whiptail
Aspidoscelis uniparens

Making a Difference

It is important to protect the valuable resources of the world, not just beautiful places like national parks.

How many of these things do you do at home? If you answered "no" to more than 10 items, talk to the grownups in your life to see if there are any household habits you might be able to change. Conserving our collective resources helps us all.

Yes	No	Do you...
☐	☐	turn off the water when you are brushing your teeth?
☐	☐	use LED light bulbs when possible?
☐	☐	use a reusable water bottle instead of disposable ones?
☐	☐	ride your bike or take the bus instead of riding in the car?
☐	☐	have a rain barrel under your roof gutters to collect rain water?
☐	☐	take quick showers?
☐	☐	avoid putting more food on your plate than you will eat?
☐	☐	take reusable lunch containers?
☐	☐	grow a garden?
☐	☐	buy items with less packaging?
☐	☐	recycle paper?
☐	☐	recycle plastic?
☐	☐	have a compost pile at home so you can make your own soil?
☐	☐	pick up trash when you see it on the trail?
☐	☐	plan a "staycation" and fly only when you have to?

| _____ | _____ |
| # of Yes | # of No |

Add up your score! Are there any "no"s that you want to turn into a yes?

Can you think of any other ways to protect our natural resources?

_____

The Ten Essentials

The ten essentials is a list of things that are important to have when you go for longer hikes. If you go on a hike to the <u>backcountry</u>, it is especially important that you have everything you need in case of an emergency. If you get lost or something unforeseen happens, it is good to be prepared to survive until help finds you.

The ten essentials list was developed in the 1930s by an outdoors group called the Mountaineers. Over time and technological advancements, this list has evolved. Can you identify all the things on the current list? Circle each of the "essentials" and cross out everything that doesn't make the cut.

fire: matches, lighter, tinder and/or stove	a pint of milk	extra money	headlamp plus extra batteries	extra clothes
extra water	a dog	Polaroid camera	bug net	lightweight games, like a deck of cards
extra food	a roll of duct tape	shelter	sun protection like sunglasses, sun-protective clothes and sunscreen	knife: plus a gear repair kit
a mirror	navigation: map, compass, altimeter, GPS device, or satellite messenger	first aid kit	extra flip-flops	entertainment like video games or books

Backcountry- a remote undeveloped rural area.

Camping Packing List

What should you take with you camping? Pretend you are in charge of your family camping trip. Make a list of what you would need to be safe and comfortable on an overnight excursion. Some considerations are listed on the side.

1.
2.
3.
4.
5.
6.
7.
8.
9.
10.
11.
12.
13.
14.
15.
16.

- What will you eat at every meal?

- What will the weather be like?

- Where will you sleep?

- What will you do during your free time?

- How luxurious do you want camp to be?

- How will you cook?

- How will you see at night?

- How will you dispose of trash?

- What might you need in case of emergencies?

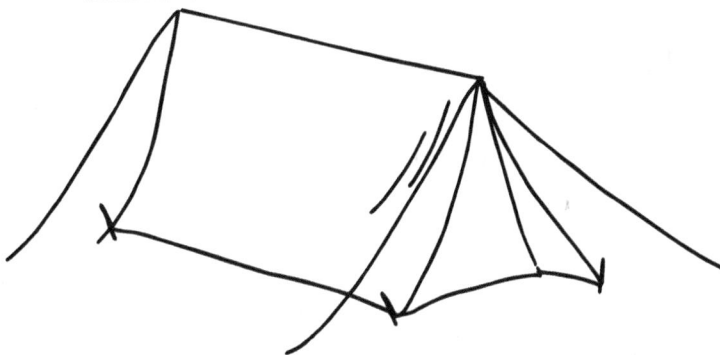

Connect the Dots #2

This animal lives in almost every state in the US, including the national park. They are nocturnal and are more active at night and sleep during the day. They are omnivorous eaters, which means they eat both plants and animals.

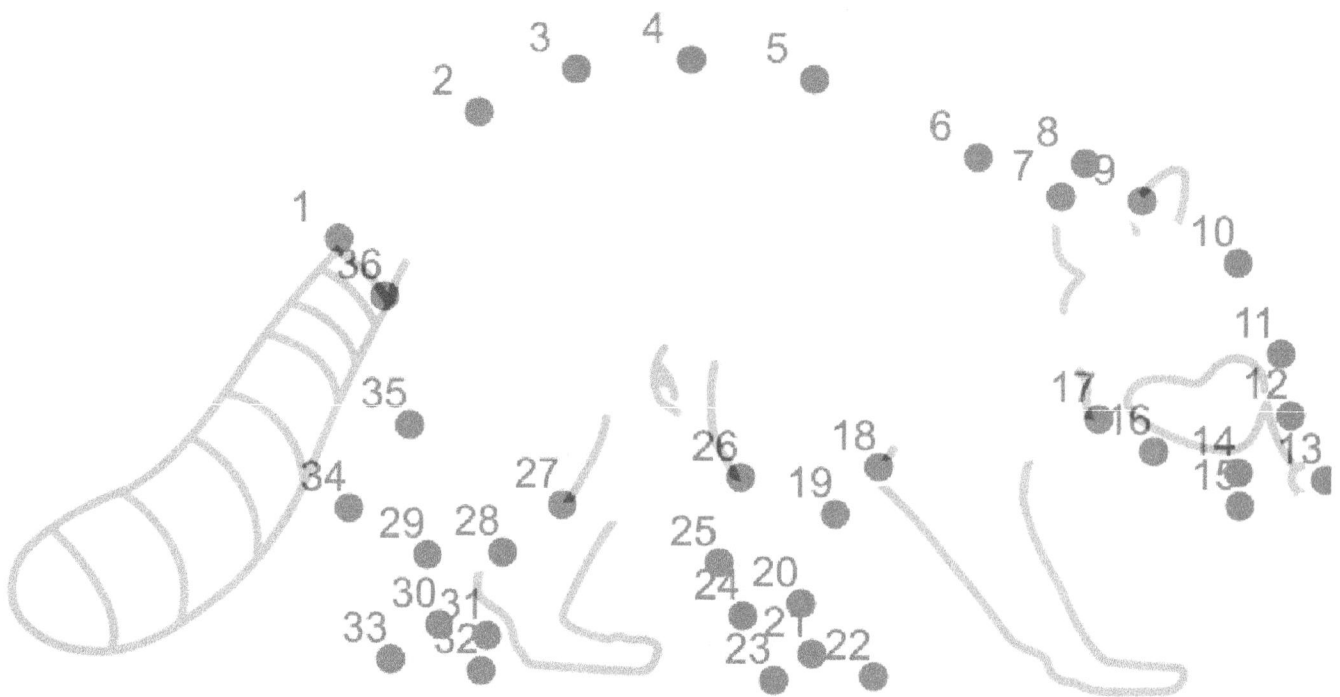

Are you an omnivore like a raccoon? An herbivore only eats plant foods. A carnivore only eats meat. An omnivore eats both. What type of eater are you? Write down some of your favorite foods to back up your answer.

_____

_____

LISTEN CAREFULLY

Visitors to Capitol Reef National Park may hear different noises from those they hear at home. Try this activity to experience this for yourself!

First, find a place outside where it is comfortable to sit or stand for a few minutes. You can do this by yourself or with a friend or family member. Once you have a good spot, close your eyes and listen. Be quiet for one minute and pay attention to what you are hearing. List some of the sounds you have heard in one of the two boxes below:

NATURAL SOUNDS
MADE BY ANIMALS, TREES OR PLANTS, THE WIND, ETC

HUMAN-MADE SOUNDS
MADE BY PEOPLE, MACHINES, ETC

ONCE YOU ARE BACK AT HOME, TRY REPEATING YOUR EXPERIMENT:

NATURAL SOUNDS
MADE BY ANIMALS, TREES OR PLANTS, THE WIND, ETC

HUMAN-MADE SOUNDS
MADE BY PEOPLE, MACHINES, ETC

WHERE DID YOU HEAR MORE NATURAL SOUNDS? _____

WHERE DID YOU HEAR MORE HUMAN SOUNDS? _____

Make Gifford Homestead Pies at Home

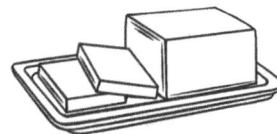

If you visit the Gifford Homestead in Fruita, you might try their famous pies made with Utah-grown fruit. The house was once lived in by Mormon pioneers and is tucked in among the cliffs in Capitol Reef National Park. The people that lived in Fruita ate what they grew, including lots of fruit.

If you can't make it to the Gifford Homestead, try making an apple pie at home! Ask an adult to help with slicing the apples and using the oven.

You can try to make your own pie crust like the settlers of Fruita did, but you can also buy a pre-made crust too.

YOU'LL NEED

- 1 (9 inch) pie shell
- 8 medium-sized, tart apples such as Granny Smith
- ¾ cup sugar
- 3 Tbs all-purpose flour
- ½ tsp ground cinnamon
- ⅛ tsp ground nutmeg
- ½ cup all-purpose flour
- ½ cup packed brown sugar
- 3 Tbs cold butter

ALL YOU HAVE TO DO

1. Core and thinly slice the apples. Add them to a large bowl.
2. In a small bowl, stir together the sugar, 3 Tbs flour, cinnamon, and nutmeg. Sprinkle mixture over apples and mix until apple slices are evenly coated. Next, add the mixture into your pre-made pie shell.
3. Preheat oven to 375 degrees Farenheit.
4. In a small bowl, mix together 1/2 cup flour and brown sugar. Cut in butter with a pastry cutter until mixture is crumbly and chunks are pea-sized. (If you do not have a pastry cutter, you can use forks or even your hands.) Sprinkle mixture over apple filling. Cover the top loosely with aluminum foil.
5. Bake in preheated oven for 25 minutes. With help, take out of the over and remove the foil. Return to the oven and bake an additional 25 to 30 minutes until the filling is bubbly and the crust is golden-brown. Cool on a wire rack.

Capitol Reef Word Search

Words may be horizontal, vertical, or diagonal
and they might be backward!

1. pie
2. utah
3. orchards
4. domes
5. cliffs
6. canyon
7. capitol gorge
8. torrey
9. red rock
10. wayne
11. dutton
12. kiln
13. silt
14. mesa verde
15. stone bridge
16. sandstone
17. waterpocket
18. Fremont River

```
F M R E W A T E R P O C K E T
E R E D R O C K O R P R O N R
O L E F A I T H F U I I N O O
W A M E S A V E R D E B T T O
A D E C M Y O T C L I F F S S
V G D S N O T T U D S O N D E
P E P K I L N S B G T A A N O
E L M A R Y O T E T E S I A R
R T P U T A H Y R R E T W S C
K S Y U L E S R T I N O S A H
L G R A I E P D R C V N T M A
A N D H S F R G R N H E O P R
T O R R E Y I O O F T B R I D
D P B N M S N Y N A M R D N S
R M Y L O R N D S C T I U G O
A A Q U D A R E L E R D M E N
W C R T C A V E R T I G E W D
C A P I T O L G O R G E A D M
```

Find the Match!
What are Baby Animals Called?

Match the animal to its baby. The first one is done for you.

Elk	eaglet
Bald Eagle	calf
Little Brown Bat	snakelets
Striped Skunk	pup
Great Horned Owl	owlet
Western Toad	kit
Mountain Lion	tadpole
Garter snake	kitten

Bird Scavenger Hunt

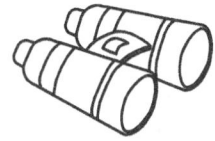

Capitol Reef National Park is a great place to go birdwatching. You don't have to be able to identify different species of birds in order to have fun. Open your eyes and tune in your ears. Check off as many birds on this list as you can.

☐ A colorful bird   ☐ A big bird

☐ A brown bird   ☐ A small bird

☐ A bird in a tree   ☐ A hopping bird

☐ A bird with long tail feathers   ☐ A flying bird

☐ A bird making noise   ☐ A bird's nest

☐ A bird eating or hunting   ☐ A bird's footprint on the ground

☐ A bird with spots   ☐ A bird with stripes somewhere on it

What was the easiest bird on the list to find? What was the hardest?
Why do you think that was?

_____

_____

_____

The Perfect Picnic Spot

Fill in the blanks on this page without looking at the full story. Once you have each line filled out, use the words you've chosen to complete the story on the next page.

EMOTION_____

FOOD_____

SOMETHING SWEET_____

STORE_____

MODE OF TRANSPORTATION_____

NOUN_____

SOMETHING ALIVE_____

SAUCE_____

PLURAL VEGETABLES_____

ADJECTIVE_____

PLURAL BODY PART_____

ANIMAL_____

PLURAL FRUIT_____

PLACE_____

SOMETHING TALL_____

COLOR_____

ADJECTIVE_____

NOUN_____

A DIFFERENT ANIMAL_____

FAMILY MEMBER #1_____

FAMILY MEMBER #2_____

VERB THAT ENDS IN -ING_____

A DIFFERENT FOOD_____

The Perfect Picnic Spot

Use the words from the previous page to complete a silly story.

When my family suggested having our lunch at the Chestnut Picnic Area, I was

_____. I love eating my _____ outside! I knew we had picked up a
EMOTION   FOOD

box of _____ from the _____ for after lunch, my favorite. We drove up
SOMETHING SWEET   STORE

to the area and I jumped out of the _____. "I will find the perfect spot for
                                  MODE OF TRANSPORTATION

a picnic!" I grabbed a _____ for us to sit on, and I ran off. I passed a picnic
                      NOUN

table, but it was covered with _____ so we couldn't sit there. The next
                            SOMETHING ALIVE

picnic table looked okay, but there were smears of _____ and pieces of
                                                SAUCE

_____ everywhere. The people that were there before must have been
PLURAL VEGETABLES

_____! I gritted my _____ together and kept walking down the path,
ADJECTIVE   PLURAL BODY PART

determined to find the perfect spot. I wanted a table with a good view of the

cliff. Why was this so hard? If we were lucky, I might even get to see _____
                                                                    ANIMAL

eating some _____ on the cliffside. They don't have those in _____ where I
          PLURAL FRUIT   PLACE

am from. I walked down a little hill and there it was, the perfect spot! The trees

towered overhead and looked as tall as _____. The patch of grass was a
                                     SOMETHING TALL

beautiful _____ color. The _____ flowers were growing on
        COLOR   ADJECTIVE

the side of a _____. I looked across the cliff edge and even saw a
            NOUN

_____ on the edge of a rock. I looked back to see my _____ and
DIFFERENT ANIMAL   FAMILY MEMBER #1

_____ _____ a picnic basket. "I hope you brought plenty of
FAMILY MEMBER #2 VERB THAT ENDS IN ING

_____, I'm starving!"
A DIFFERENT FOOD

29

Hike to a Hoodoo

start here →

DID YOU KNOW?
Hoodoos are tall, thin rocks that protrude from the bottom of a basin. Have you seen any in the park?

Utah Word Search

Words may be horizontal, vertical, or diagonal
and they might be backward!

1. osprey
2. Utah
3. southwest
4. canyon
5. explore
6. reptile
7. dry
8. desert
9. hiking
10. rocks
11. Salt Lake City
12. geology
13. pinyon pine
14. pine nuts
15. cliffs
16. beehive
17. arid
18. cactus

```
C W S O U T H W E S T L O W K
H T A A K I L O C H E L A N J
T G E O L O G Y C C L B A P E
P M P A Y T R S C E R L H L X
I I A D R A L L O E I U I A P
N O N D D I R A D C T T K S L
Y E S E E H E K K B P R I C O
O L B A N U I E G E N E N A R
N E H S G U L O R E C D G D E
P C I C A C T U S H P I O E A
I T A L C H I S O I K E T S N
N R N I K O E I O V O K I Y E
E I O F H Z D E S E R T L G W
J C G F L O V E P O O R V E H
N I L S K H I N R O C K S E A
X T A I A E E G E Z E P R N L
H T D T O E N O Y N A C C I E
U J U O S N E D N Y M A L A Z
```

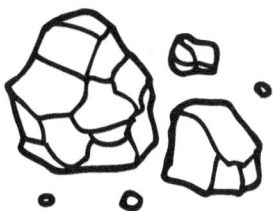

31

Leave No Trace Quiz

Leave No Trace is a concept that helps people make decisions during outdoor recreation that protects the environment. There are seven principles that guide us when we spend time outdoors, whether you are in a national park or not. Are you an expert in Leave No Trace? Take this quiz and find out!

1. How can you plan ahead and prepare to ensure you have the best experience you can in the national park?
    a. Make sure you stop by the ranger station for a map and to ask about current conditions.
    b. Just wing it! You will know the best trail when you see it.
    c. Stick to your plan, even if conditions change. You traveled a long way to get here, and you should stick to your plan.
2. What is an example of traveling on a durable surface?
    a. Walking only on the designated path.
    b. Walking on the grass that borders the trail if the trail is very muddy.
    c. Taking a shortcut if you can find one since it means you will be walking less.
3. Why should you dispose of waste properly?
    a. You don't need to. Park rangers love to pick up the trash you leave behind.
    b. You actually should leave your leftovers behind, because animals will eat them. It is important to make sure they aren't hungry.
    c. So that other peoples' experiences of the park are not impacted by you leaving your waste behind.
4. How can you best follow the concept "leave what you find"?
    a. Take only a small rock or leaf to remember your trip.
    b. Take pictures, but leave any physical items where they are.
    c. Leave everything you find, unless it may be rare like an arrowhead, then it is okay to take.
5. What is not a good example of minimizing campfire impacts?
    a. Only having a campfire in a pre-existing campfire ring.
    b. Checking in with current conditions when you consider making a campfire.
    c. Building a new campfire ring in a location that has a better view.
6. What is a poor example of respecting wildlife?
    a. Building squirrel houses out of rocks so the squirrels have a place to live.
    b. Stay far away from wildlife and give them plenty of space.
    c. Reminding your grown-ups to not drive too fast in animal habitats while visiting the park.
7. How can you show consideration of other visitors?
    a. Play music on your speaker so other people at the campground can enjoy it.
    b. Wear headphones on the trail if you choose to listen to music.
    c. Make sure to yell "Hello!" to every animal you see at top volume.

Park Poetry

America's parks inspire art of all kinds. Painters, sculptors, photographers, writers, and artists of all mediums have taken inspiration from natural beauty. They have turned their inspiration into great works.

Use this space to write your own poem about the park. Think about what you have experienced or seen. Use descriptive language to create an acrostic poem. This type of poem has the first letter of each line spell out another word. Create an acrostic that spells out the word "Utah."

U _____

T _____

A _____

H _____

Under big sky

Towering rocks

All around me

Hot dry land

Up in the air

Top predator

A bird so ferocious

Hovering over its prey

Photobook

Draw some pictures of
things you saw in the park.

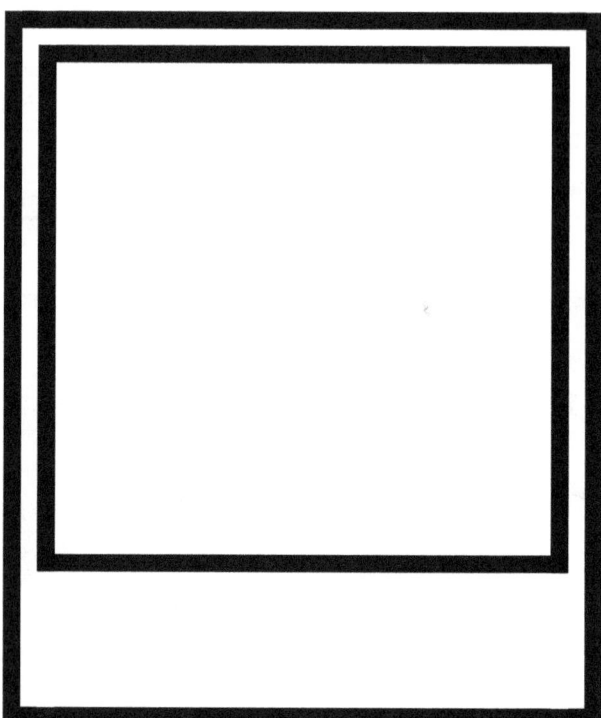

Catch a Fish in the Fremont River

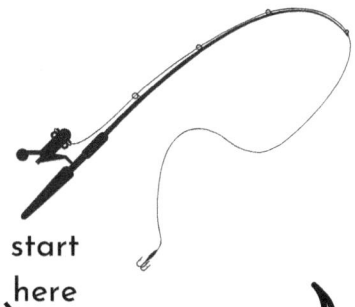

start here

Grab a fishing pole and try to reel in a fish.

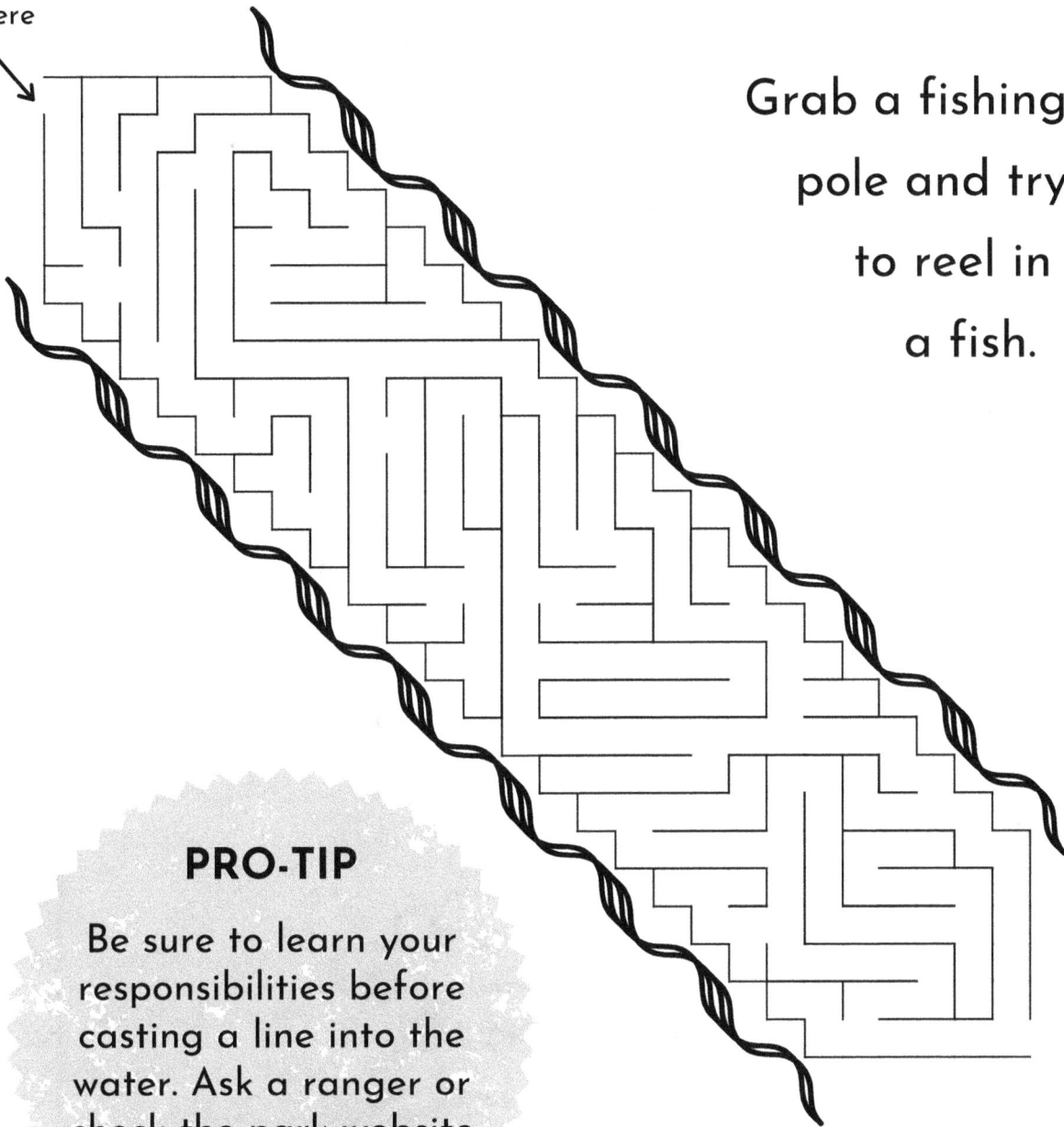

PRO-TIP

Be sure to learn your responsibilities before casting a line into the water. Ask a ranger or check the park website before you go.

Stacking Rocks

Have you ever seen stacks of rocks while hiking in national parks? Do you know what they are or what they mean? These rock piles are called cairns and often mark hiking routes in parks. Every park has a different way to maintain trails and cairns. However, they all have the same rule: If you come across a cairn, do not disturb it.

Color the cairn and the rules to remember.

1. Do not tamper with cairns.

If a cairn is tampered with or an unauthorized one is built, then future visitors may become disoriented or even lost.

2. Do not build unauthorized cairns.

Moving rocks disturbs the soil and makes the area more prone to erosion. Disturbing rocks can disturb fragile plants.

3. Do not add to existing cairns.

Authorized cairns are carefully designed. Adding to them can actually cause them to collapse.

Decoding Using American Sign Language

American Sign Language, also called ASL for short, is a language that many Deaf people or people who are hard of hearing use to communicate. People use ASL to communicate with their hands. Did you know people from all over the country and world travel to national parks? You may hear people speaking other languages. You might also see people using ASL. Use the American Manual Alphabet chart to decode some national parks facts.

This was the first national park to be established:

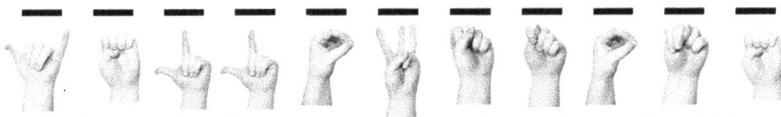

_ _ _ _ _ _ _ _ _ _

This is the biggest national park in the US:

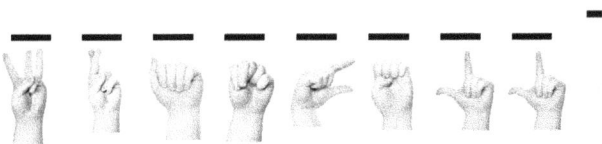

_ _ _ _ _ _ _ _ -

_ _ . _ _

This is the most visited national park:

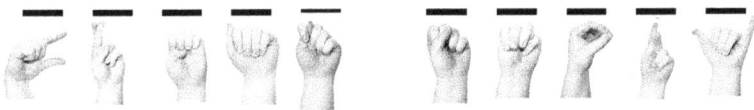

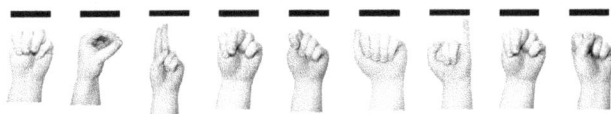

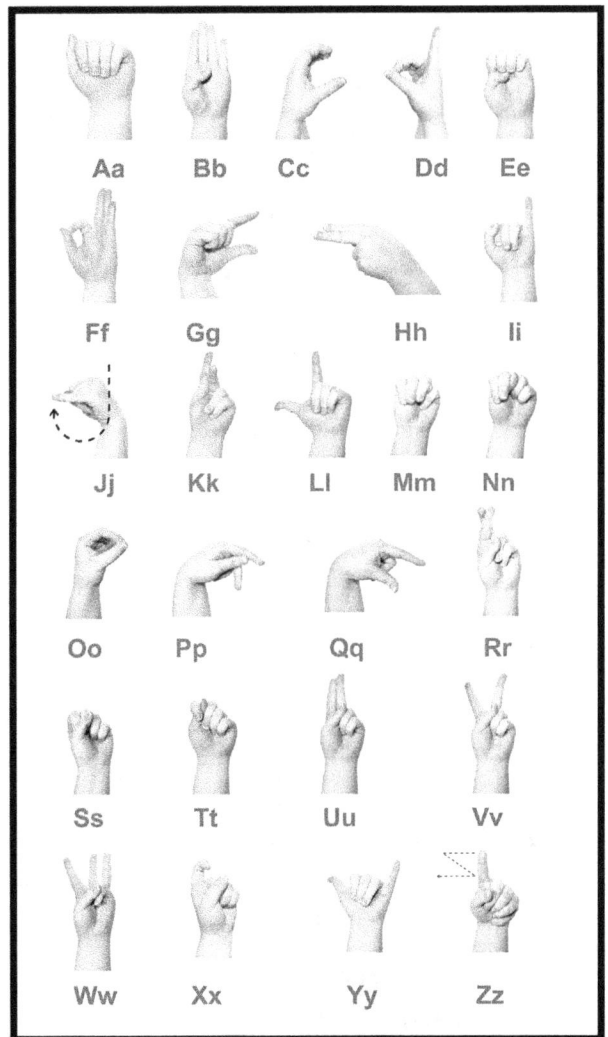

_ _ _ _ _ _ _ _

_ _ _ _ _ _ _ _

Aa	Bb	Cc	Dd	Ee
Ff	Gg		Hh	Ii
Jj	Kk	Ll	Mm	Nn
Oo	Pp		Qq	Rr
Ss	Tt		Uu	Vv
Ww	Xx		Yy	Zz

Hint: Pay close attention to the position of the thumb!

Try it! Using the chart, try to make the letters of the alphabet with your hand. What is the hardest letter to make? Can you spell out your name? Show a friend or family member and have them watch you spell out the name of the national park you are in.

Go Horseback Riding in the Cathedral Valley District

Help find the horse's lost shoe!

start here

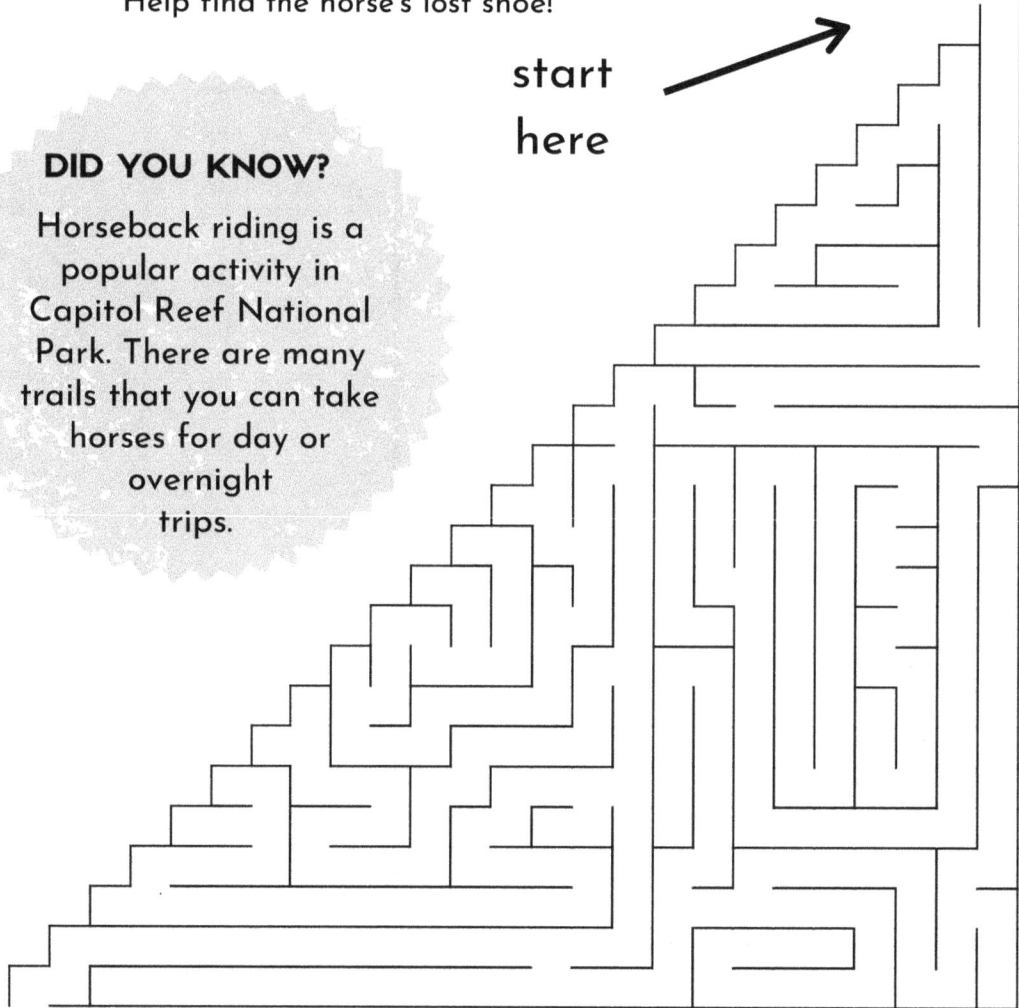

Butterflies of the Utah Desert

Dozens of species of butterflies and moths live in Capitol Reef National Park. Their wingspan size varies, as do the patterns on their wings. Design your own butterfly below. Make sure the wings are symmetrical, meaning both sides match.

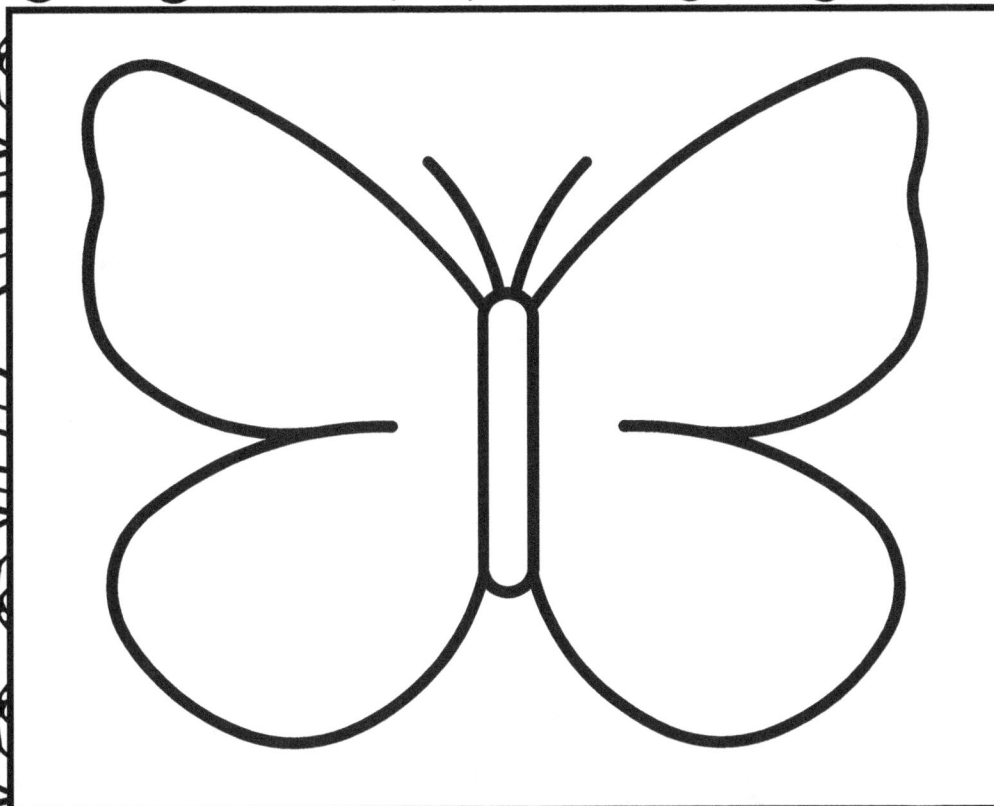

A Hike to Sunset Point

Fill in the blanks on this page without looking at the full story. Once you have each line filled out, use the words you've chosen to complete the story on the next page.

ADJECTIVE _____

SOMETHING TO EAT _____

SOMETHING TO DRINK _____

NOUN _____

ARTICLE OF CLOTHING _____

BODY PART _____

VERB _____

ANIMAL _____

SAME TYPE OF FOOD _____

ADJECTIVE _____

SAME ANIMAL _____

VERB THAT ENDS IN "ED" _____

NUMBER _____

A DIFFERENT NUMBER _____

SOMETHING THAT FLIES _____

LIGHT SOURCE _____

PLURAL NOUN _____

FAMILY MEMBER _____

YOUR NICKNAME _____

A Hike to Sunset Point

Use the words from the previous page to complete a silly story.

I went for a hike to Sunset Point today. In my favorite _____ backpack, I
                                                    ADJECTIVE

made sure to pack a map so I wouldn't get lost. I also threw in an extra

_____ just in case I got hungry and a bottle of _____. I put
SOMETHING TO EAT   SOMETHING TO DRINK

on my _____ spray, and a tied a _____ around my
        NOUN   ARTICLE OF CLOTHING

_____, in case it gets chilly. I started to _____ down the path. As
BODY PART   VERB

soon as I turned the corner, I came face to face with a(n) _____. I think
                                                            ANIMAL

it was as startled as I was! What should I do? I had to think fast! Should I

give it some of my _____? No. I had to remember what the
                    SAME TYPE OF FOOD

_____ ranger told me. "If you see one, back away slowly and try not to
ADJECTIVE

scare it." Soon enough, the _____ _____ away. The coast
                              SAME ANIMAL   VERB THAT ENDS IN ED

was clear. _____ hours later, I finally got to the lookout. I felt like I could
            NUMBER

see for a _____ miles. I took a picture of a _____ so I could always
          A DIFFERENT NUMBER   NOUN

remember this moment. As I was putting my camera away, a _____
                                                          SOMETHING THAT FLIES

flew by, reminding me that it was almost nighttime. I turned on my

_____ and headed back. I could hear the _____ singing their
LIGHT SOURCE   PLURAL INSECT

evening song. Just as I was getting tired, I saw my _____ and our tent.
                                                      FAMILY MEMBER

"Welcome back _____! How was your hike?"
                NICKNAME

Protecting the Park

When you visit national parks, it is important to leave the park the way you found it. Did you know that the national parks get hundreds of millions of visitors every year? We can only protect national parks for future visitors to enjoy if everyone does their part. The choices that each visitor makes when visiting the park have a big impact all together.

Read each line below. Write a sentence or draw a picture to show the impacts these changes would make on the park.

What would happen if every visitor fed the wild animals?

What would happen if every visitor picked a flower?

What would happen if every visitor took home a few rocks?

What would happen if every visitor wrote or carved their name on the rocks or trees?

Let's Go Camping
Word Search

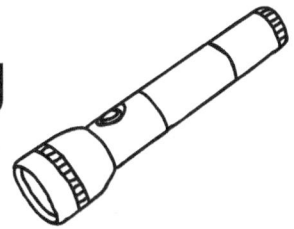

Words may be horizontal, vertical, or diagonal and they might be backward!

1. tent
2. camp stove
3. sleeping bag
4. bug spray
5. sunscreen
6. map
7. flashlight
8. pillow
9. lantern
10. ice
11. snacks
12. smores
13. water
14. first aid kit
15. chair
16. cards
17. books
18. games
19. trail
20. hat

```
D P P I L L O W D B T E A C I
E O A D P R E A A M B R C A N
P W C A M P S T O V E I H X G
R A H S G E L E B E E D A P S
E L B U G S P R A Y N G I E A
S I A H G C I C N N M E R C N
C W N L A F I R S K O O B F K
M T A E M I L E L H M R W L J
T A P R E A O R E S L B A A B
S M P A S R R T E N T L U S C
C E A I I R C G P E I U J H A
S S N A C K S S I M O K I L R
I J R S F O I S N J R A Q I D
C Y E T L E V E G U O R V G S
E W T A K C A B B S S O H H M
X J N F I R S T A I D K I T T
U A A E S S E N G E T P V A B
C J L I A R T D N A M A H A S
```

43

All in the Day of a Park Ranger

Park Rangers are hardworking individuals dedicated to protecting our parks, monuments, museums, and more. They take care of the natural and cultural resources for future generations. Rangers also help protect the visitors of the park. Their responsibilities are broad and they work both with the public and behind the scenes.

What have you seen park rangers do? Use your knowledge of the duties of park rangers to fill out a typical daily schedule, one activity for each hour. Feel free to make up your own, but some examples of activities are provided on the right. Read carefully, not all of the example activities are befitting a ranger!

Time	Activity
6 am	Lead a sunrise hike
7 am	
8 am	
9 am	
10 am	
11 am	
12 pm	Enjoy a lunch break outside
1 pm	
2 pm	
3 pm	
4 pm	Teach visitors about the geology of the area
5 pm	
6 pm	
7 pm	
8 pm	
9 pm	

- feed the golden eagles
- build trails for visitors to enjoy
- throw rocks off the side of the mountain
- rescue lost hikers
- study animal behavior
- record air quality data
- answer questions at the visitor center
- pick wildflowers
- pick up litter
- share marshmallows with squirrels
- repair handrails
- lead a class on a field trip
- catch toads and make them race
- lead people on educational hikes
- write articles for the park website
- protect the river from pollution
- remove non-native plants from the park
- study how climate change is affecting the park
- give a talk about the Waterpocket Fold
- lead a program for campers on bighorn sheep

If you were a park ranger, which of the above tasks would you enjoy most?

_____

_____

44

Draw Yourself as a Park Ranger

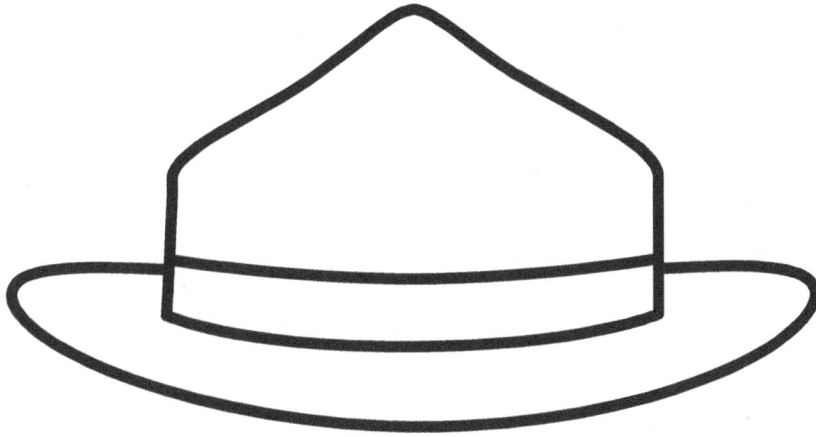

RANGER

Fish at Capitol Reef

Unscramble these common fish names that live in the park.

1.
SUCKER

2.
OTRTU

3.
CADE

4.
SPINLUC

5.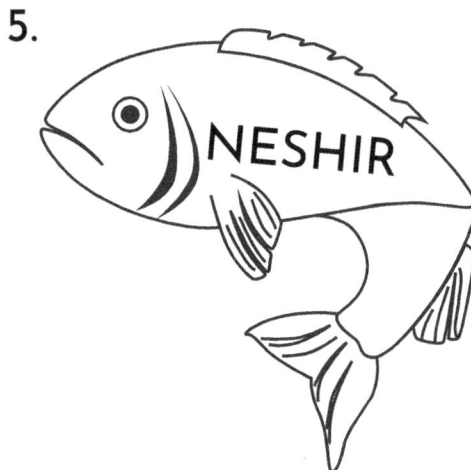
NESHIR

1. _____
2. _____
3. _____
4. _____
5. _____

Word Bank

dace
sunfish
trout
minnow
sculpin
shiner
whitefish
sucker

Amphibians

Two species of toad and two species of frogs live in Capitol Reef National Park. Frogs and toads both spend the beginning of their lives the same way, as tadpoles. Tadpoles hatch from eggs in water, usually in springs or pools of water.

Both frogs and toads are amphibians. Color the amphibians below.

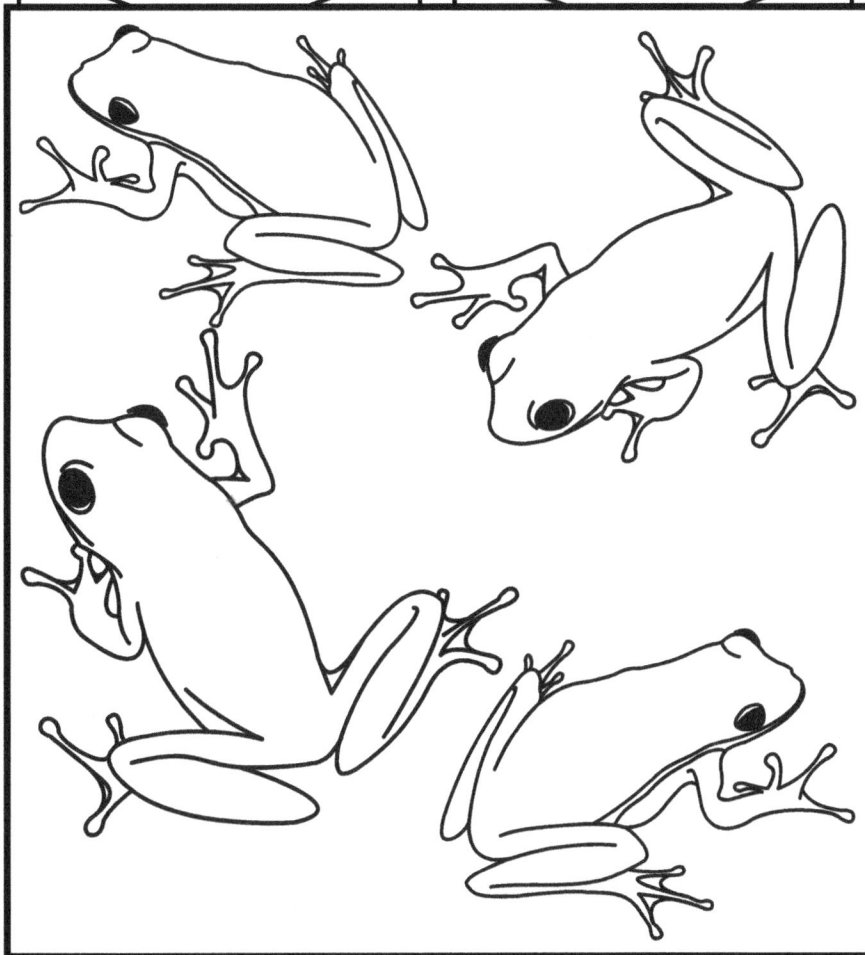

Being Respectful

Rangers need your help! Some people toss their trash where they shouldn't, create graffiti, or take artifacts when they visit Capitol Reef National Park. Create a poster to help show other visitors how to be respectful in the space below.

It is important to take precautions to stay safe outdoors, especially when it is very hot outside. When someone gets overheated or dehydrated, they may feel sick or even require medical attention.

Use the cryptogram below to decode three tips on how to prevent heat-related illnesses. You may need to do some math to figure out the answers.

T __ __ __   __ __ __ __ __ __   __ __   __ __ __ __
12   5   12/2   50   30   21   50   5   2x3   36   3x4   27   21   50   6x6   12

__ __   __ __ __   __ __ __ __ __ .
99   10   15-3   4   50   36   7-3   5   1   50

__ __ __ __   H __ __ __ __ __ __ __   __ __
36   12   1x5   18   4   2x9   1   21   5   12   50   8-7   30   18

__ __ __ __ __ __ __ __   __ __ __ __   __ __ __ __ __ __ __ .
1   21   99   10   6   33x3   10   75   35   3x9   12   36   27   5x5   18/2   5   12   50   21

__ __ A __   __ __ __ __ __ __ __ __ __   __ __ __
9   50   12-7   21   36   3   10   36   15   21   5x10   50   10   5   10   12-11

__ __ __ - __ __ __ __ __ __ __ __ __
36   3   10   8   7x3   27   12   50   15   9+3   99   80   50

__ __ __ __ __ __ I N G .
15   35   27   12   2x2   99   10   75

a	b	c	d	e	f	g	h	i	j	k	l	m	n	o
5	30	15	1	50	25	75	4	99	20	6	35	49	10	27

p	q	r	s	t	u	v	w	x	y	z
8	16	21	36	12	3	80	9	40	18	7

63 National Parks

How many other national parks have you been to? Which one do you want to visit next? Note that some of these parks fall on the border of more than one state, you may check it off more than once!

Alaska
- [ ] Denali National Park
- [ ] Gates of the Arctic National Park
- [ ] Glacier Bay National Park
- [ ] Katmai National Park
- [ ] Kenai Fjords National Park
- [ ] Kobuk Valley National Park
- [ ] Lake Clark National Park
- [ ] Wrangell-St. Elias National Park

American Samoa
- [ ] National Park of American Samoa

Arizona
- [ ] Grand Canyon National Park
- [ ] Petrified Forest National Park
- [ ] Saguaro National Park

Arkansas
- [ ] Hot Springs National Park

California
- [ ] Channel Islands National Park
- [ ] Death Valley National Park
- [ ] Joshua Tree National Park
- [ ] Kings Canyon National Park
- [ ] Lassen Volcanic National Park
- [ ] Pinnacles National Park
- [ ] Redwood National Park
- [ ] Sequoia National Park
- [ ] Yosemite National Park

Colorado
- [ ] Black Canyon of the Gunnison National Park
- [ ] Great Sand Dunes National Park
- [ ] Mesa Verde National Park
- [ ] Rocky Mountain National Park

Florida
- [ ] Biscayne National Park
- [ ] Dry Tortugas National Park
- [ ] Everglades National Park

Hawaii
- [ ] Haleakalā National Park
- [ ] Hawai'i Volcanoes National Park

Idaho
- [ ] Yellowstone National Park

Kentucky
- [ ] Mammoth Cave National Park

Indiana
- [ ] Indiana Dunes National Park

Maine
- [ ] Acadia National Park

Michigan
- [ ] Isle Royale National Park

Minnesota
- [ ] Voyageurs National Park

Missouri
- [ ] Gateway Arch National Park

Montana
- [ ] Glacier National Park
- [ ] Yellowstone National Park

Nevada
- [ ] Death Valley National Park
- [ ] Great Basin National Park

New Mexico
- [ ] Carlsbad Caverns National Park
- [ ] White Sands National Park

North Dakota
- [ ] Theodore Roosevelt National Park

North Carolina
- [ ] Great Smoky Mountains National Park

Ohio
- [ ] Cuyahoga Valley National Park

Oregon
- [ ] Crater Lake National Park

South Carolina
- [ ] Congaree National Park

South Dakota
- [ ] Badlands National Park
- [ ] Wind Cave National Park

Tennessee
- [ ] Great Smoky Mountains National Park

Texas
- [ ] Big Bend National Park
- [ ] Guadalupe Mountains National Park

Utah
- [ ] Arches National Park
- [ ] Bryce Canyon National Park
- [ ] Canyonlands National Park
- [ ] Capitol Reef National Park
- [ ] Zion National Park

Virgin Islands
- [ ] Virgin Islands National Park

Virginia
- [ ] Shenandoah National Park

Washington
- [ ] Mount Rainier National Park
- [ ] North Cascades National Park
- [ ] Olympic National Park

West Virginia
- [ ] New River Gorge National Park

Wyoming
- [ ] Grand Teton National Park
- [ ] Yellowstone National Park

Other National Parks

Besides Capitol Reef National Park, there are 62 other diverse and beautiful national parks across the United States. Try your hand at this crossword. If you need help, look at the previous page for some hints.

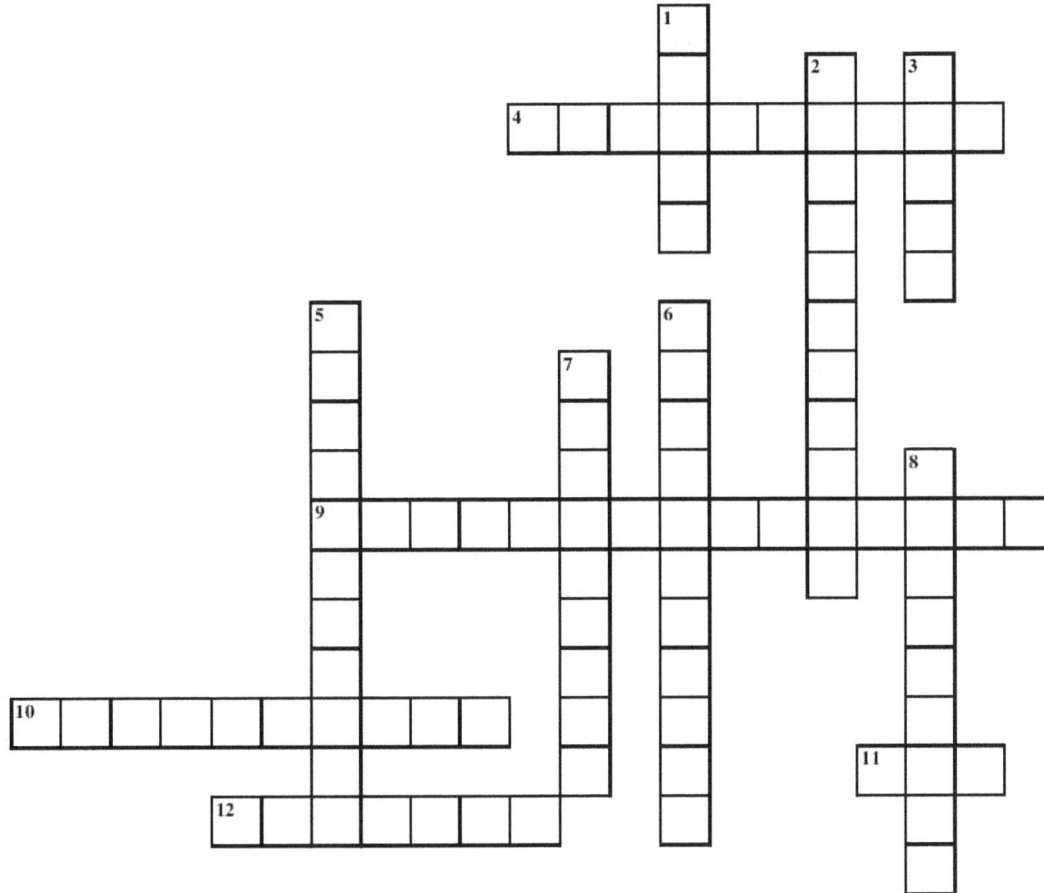

Down

1. State where Acadia National Park is located
2. This national park has the Spanish word for turtle in it.
3. Number of national parks in Alaska
5. This national park has some of the hottest temperatures in the world.
6. This national park is the only one in Idaho.
7. This toothsome creature can be famously found in Everglades National Park.
8. Only president with a national park named for them

Across

4. This state has the most national parks.
9. This park has some of the newest land in the US, caused by volcanic eruptions.
10. This park has the deepest lake in the United States.
11. This color shows up in the name of a national park in California.
12. This national park deserves a gold medal.

Which National Park Will You Go to Next?
Word Search

1. Zion
2. Big Bend
3. Glacier
4. Olympic
5. Sequoia
6. Bryce
7. Mesa Verde
8. Biscayne
9. Wind Cave
10. Great Basin
11. Katmai
12. Yellowstone
13. Voyageurs
14. Arches
15. Badlands
16. Denali
17. Glacier Bay
18. Hot Springs

```
F  M  M  E  S  A  V  E  R  D  E  B  N  E  Y
E  A  B  I  G  B  E  N  D  E  S  A  S  E  M
Y  L  I  C  A  L  O  Y  N  E  E  D  L  T  G
D  M  G  A  S  S  A  U  C  N  R  L  U  E  R
C  E  L  I  I  T  S  C  R  E  O  A  A  K  E
S  N  A  W  Y  E  E  O  I  W  T  N  A  C  A
G  I  C  H  A  A  Q  C  S  E  M  D  N  S  T
N  O  I  Z  P  R  U  T  I  M  R  S  N  E  B
I  W  E  L  M  P  O  N  B  W  E  B  K  H  A
R  J  R  F  D  N  I  F  L  I  H  B  U  C  S
P  A  B  E  E  S  A  N  E  S  O  P  W  R  I
S  J  A  E  N  Y  A  C  S  I  B  A  U  A  N
T  C  Y  I  A  D  O  H  H  Y  M  E  A  L  R
O  T  A  T  L  M  L  E  S  E  G  R  W  R  J
H  S  T  O  I  K  A  T  M  A  I  R  O  P  B
I  C  H  U  R  C  O  L  Y  M  P  I  C  O  U
O  Y  G  T  S  D  E  O  S  B  R  Y  C  E  T
W  I  N  D  C  A  V  E  I  N  R  O  H  E  M
```

52

Field Notes

Spend some time to reflect on your trip to Capitol Reef National Park. Your field notes will help you remember the things you experienced. Use the space below to write about your day.

While I was at Capitol Reef National Park...

I saw:

_____

_____

_____

_____

I heard:

_____

_____

_____

_____

I felt:

_____

Draw a picture of your favorite thing in the park.

_____

_____

I wondered:

_____

_____

_____

_____

_____

ANSWER KEY

National Park Emblem Answers

1. This represents all plants. **Sequoia Tree**

2. This represents all animals. **Bison**

3. This symbol represents the landscapes. **Mountains**

4. This represents the waters protected by the park service. **Water**

5. This represents the historical and archeological values. **Arrowhead**

Jumbles Answers

1. STAR GAZING

2. HIKING

3. BIRDING

4. CAMPING

5. PICNICKING

6. SIGHTSEEING

7. HORSEBACK RIDING

Go Birdwatching at Fruita

start here →

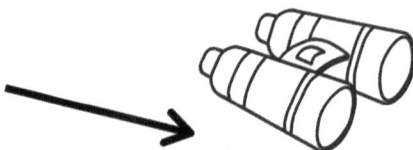

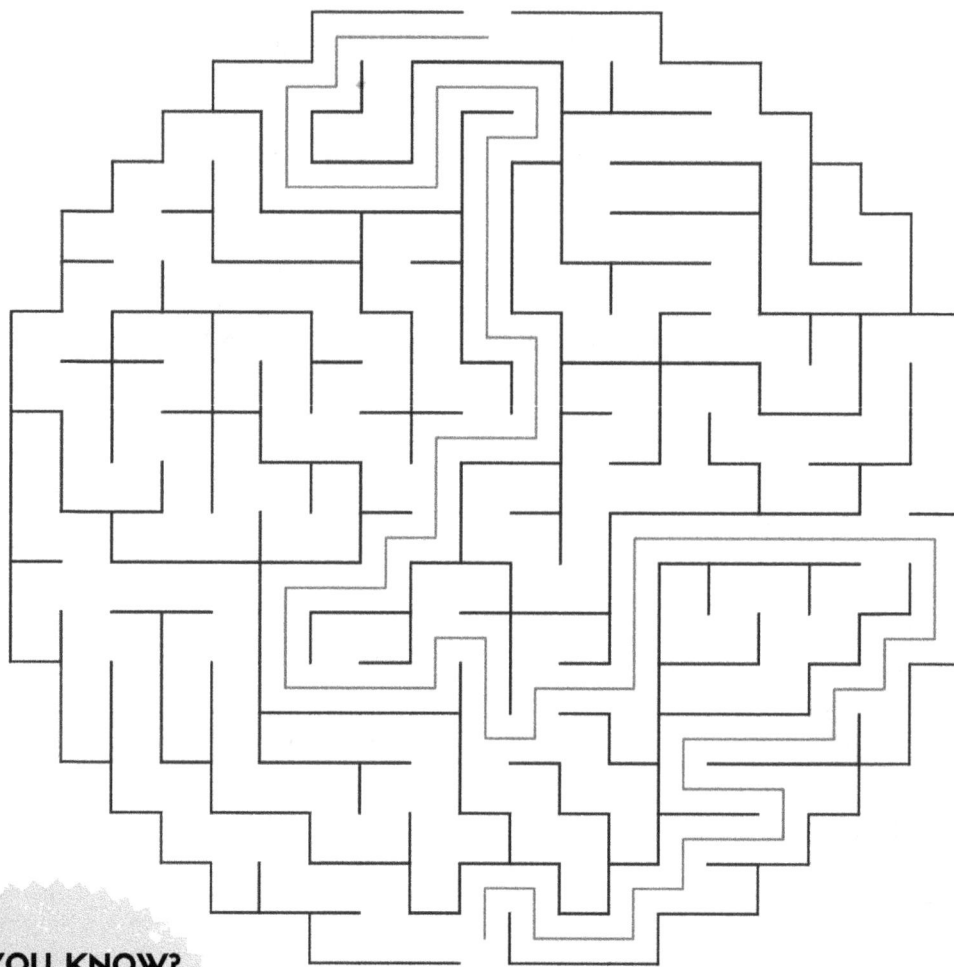

DID YOU KNOW?
Capitol Reef NP is home to several birds of prey, including eagles, hawks, and owls. Birds of prey are birds that hunt other animals for food.

Answers: Who Lives in Capitol Reef?

Here are some plants and animals that live in the park. Use the word bank to fill in the clues below. Pay attention to how many letters each word has to see where it fits.

GOPHER ■ S NAKE

B O BCAT

MU LE ■ DEER

COT T ONTAIL

W H IPTAIL

CANYON ■ W REN

PRICKLY ■ P E AR

O S PREY

CHEA T GRASS

WORD BANK:

CHEATGRASS, GOPHER SNAKE, BOBCAT, CANYON WREN, MULE DEER, PRICKLY PEAR, COTTONTAIL, OSPREY, WHIPTAIL

Find the Match!
Common Names and Latin Names

Match the common name to the scientific name for each animal. The first one is done for you. Use clues on the page before and after this one to complete the matches.

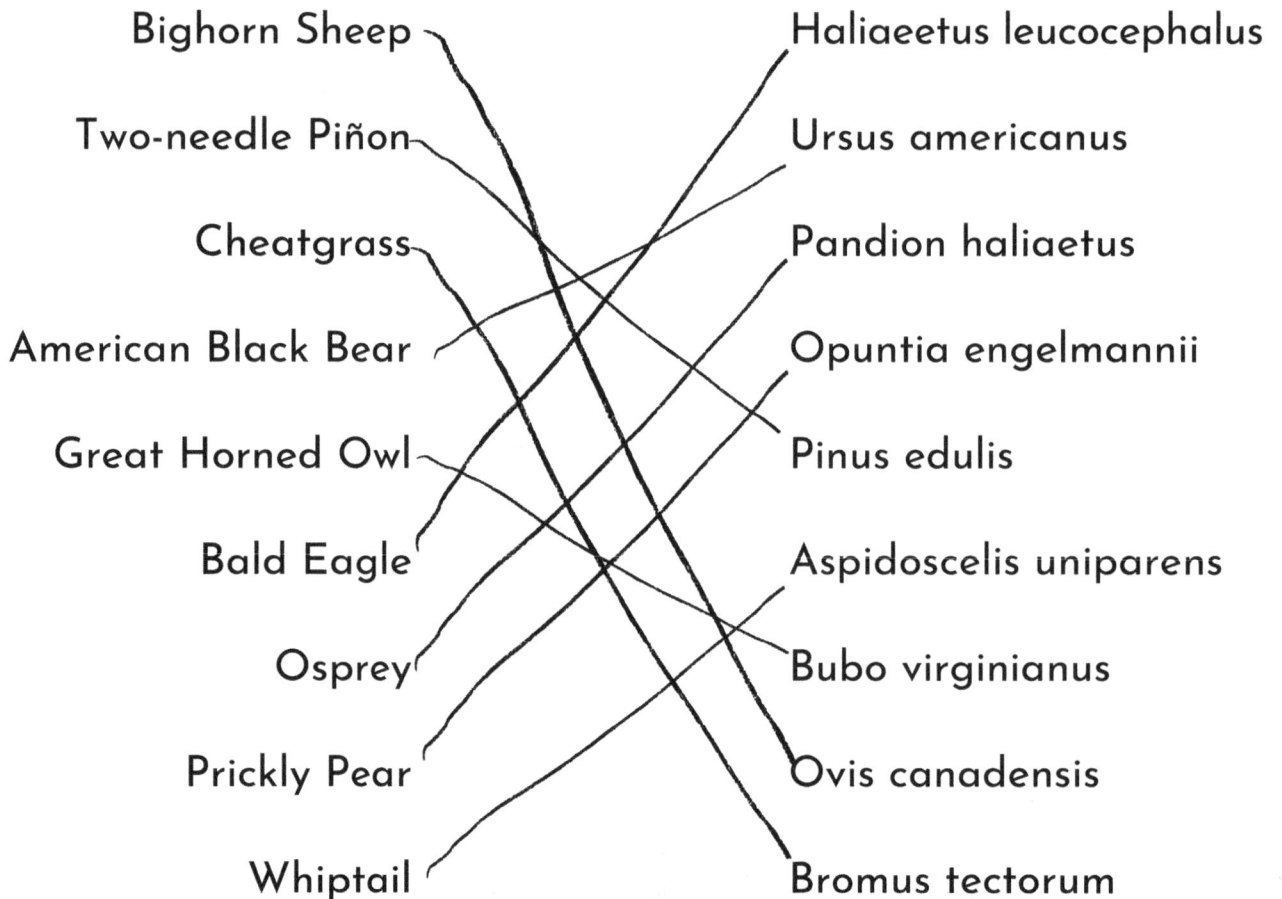

Bighorn Sheep   Haliaeetus leucocephalus

Two-needle Piñon   Ursus americanus

Cheatgrass   Pandion haliaetus

American Black Bear   Opuntia engelmannii

Great Horned Owl   Pinus edulis

Bald Eagle   Aspidoscelis uniparens

Osprey   Bubo virginianus

Prickly Pear   Ovis canadensis

Whiptail   Bromus tectorum

Bald Eagle

Haliaeetus leucocephalus

Answers: The Ten Essentials

The ten essentials is a list of things that are important to have when you go for longer hikes. If you go on a hike to the <u>backcountry</u>, it is especially important that you have everything you need in case of an emergency. If you get lost or something unforeseen happens, it is good to be prepared to survive until help finds you.

The ten essentials list was developed in the 1930s by an outdoors group called the Mountaineers. Over time and technological advancements, this list has evolved. Can you identify all the things on the current list? Circle each of the "essentials" and cross out everything that doesn't make the cut.

(fire: matches, lighter, tinder and/or stove)	~~a pint of milk~~	~~extra money~~	(headlamp plus extra batteries)	(extra clothes)
(extra water)	~~a dog~~	~~Polaroid camera~~	~~bug net~~	~~lightweight games like a deck of cards~~
(extra food)	~~a roll of duct tape~~	(shelter)	(sun protection like sunglasses, sun-protective clothes and sunscreen)	(knife: plus a gear repair kit)
~~a mirror~~	(navigation: map, compass, altimeter, GPS device, or satellite messenger)	(first aid kit)	~~extra flip-flops~~	~~entertainment like video games or books~~

Backcountry- a remote undeveloped rural area.

Capitol Reef Word Search

Words may be horizontal, vertical, or diagonal
and they might be backward!

1. pie
2. utah
3. orchards
4. domes
5. cliffs
6. canyon
7. capitol gorge
8. torrey
9. red rock
10. wayne
11. dutton
12. kiln
13. silt
14. mesa verde
15. stone bridge
16. sandstone
17. waterpocket
18. Fremont River

```
F M R E W A T E R P O C K E T
E R E D R O C K O R P R O N R
O L E F A I T H F U I I N O O
W A M E S A V E R D E B T T O
A D E C M Y O T C L I F F S S
V G D S N O T T U D S O N D E
P E P K I L N S B G T A A N O
E L M A R Y O T E T E S I A R
R T P U T A H Y R R E T W S C
K S Y U L E S R T I N O S A H
L G R A I E P D R C V N T M A
A N D H S F R G R N H E O P R
T O R R E Y I O O F T B R I D
D P B N M S N Y N A M R D N S
R M Y L O R N D S C T I U G O
A A Q U D A R E L E R D M E N
W C R T C A V E R T I G E W D
C A P I T O L G O R G E A D M
```

60

Answers: Find the Match!
What are Baby Animals Called?

Match the animal to its baby. The first one is done for you.

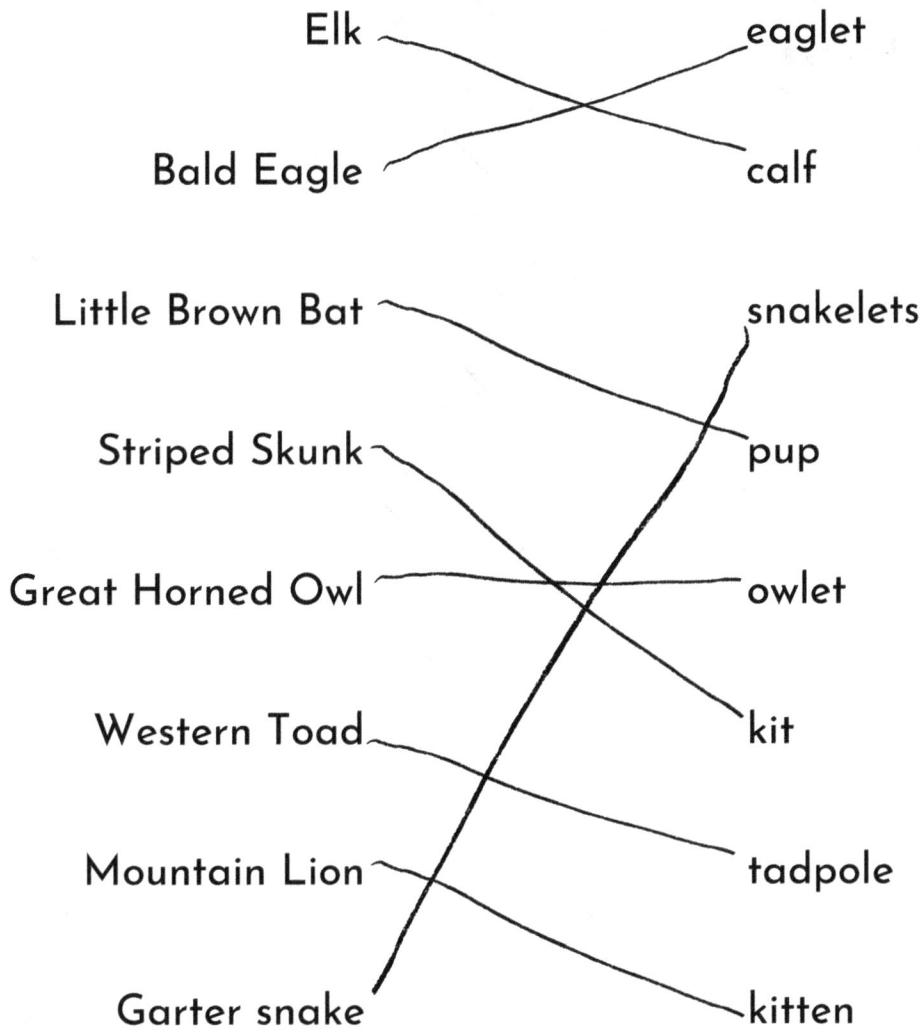

Elk   eaglet

Bald Eagle   calf

Little Brown Bat   snakelets

Striped Skunk   pup

Great Horned Owl   owlet

Western Toad   kit

Mountain Lion   tadpole

Garter snake   kitten

Answer: Hike to a Hoodoo

start here →

DID YOU KNOW?
Hoodoos are tall, thin rocks that protrude from the bottom of a basin. Have you seen any in the park?

Utah Word Search

Words may be horizontal, vertical, or diagonal
and they might be backward!

1. osprey
2. Utah
3. southwest
4. canyon
5. explore
6. reptile
7. dry
8. desert
9. hiking
10. rocks
11. Salt Lake City
12. geology
13. pinyon pine
14. pine nuts
15. cliffs
16. beehive
17. arid
18. cactus

```
C W S O U T H W E S T L O W K
H T A A K I L O C H E L A N J
T G E O L O G Y C C L B A P E
P M P A Y T R S C E R L H L X
I I A D R A L L O E I U I A P
N O N D D I R A D C T T K S L
Y E S E H E K K B P R I C O R
O L B A N U I E G E N E N A R
N E H S G U L O R E C D G D E
P C I C A C T U S H P I O E A
I T A L C H I S O I K E T S N
N R N I K O E I O V O K I Y E
E I O F H Z D E S E R T L G W
J C G F L O V E P O O R V E H
N I L S K H I N R O C K S E A
X T A I A E E G E Z E P R N L
H T D T O E N O Y N A C C I E
U J U O S N E D N Y M A L A Z
```

63

Answers: Leave No Trace Quiz

Leave No Trace is a concept that helps people make decisions during outdoor recreation that protects the environment. There are seven principles that guide us when we spend time outdoors, whether you are in a national park or not. Are you an expert in Leave No Trace? Take this quiz and find out!

1. How can you plan ahead and prepare to ensure you have the best experience you can in the National Park?

    A. Make sure you stop by the ranger station for a map and to ask about current conditions.

2. What is an example of traveling on a durable surface?

    A. Walking only on the designated path.

3. Why should you dispose of waste properly?

    C. So that other peoples' experiences of the park are not impacted by you leaving your waste behind.

4. How can you best follow the concept "leave what you find"?

    B. Take pictures but leave any physical items where they are.

5. What is not a good example of minimizing campfire impacts?

    C. Building a new campfire ring in a location that has a better view.

6. What is a poor example of respecting wildlife?

    A. Building squirrel houses out of rocks from the river so the squirrels have a place to live.

7. How can you show consideration of other visitors?

    B. Wear headphones on the trail if you choose to listen to music.

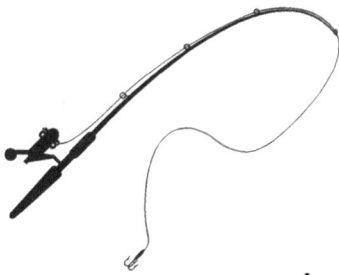

Solution: Catch a Fish in the Fremont River

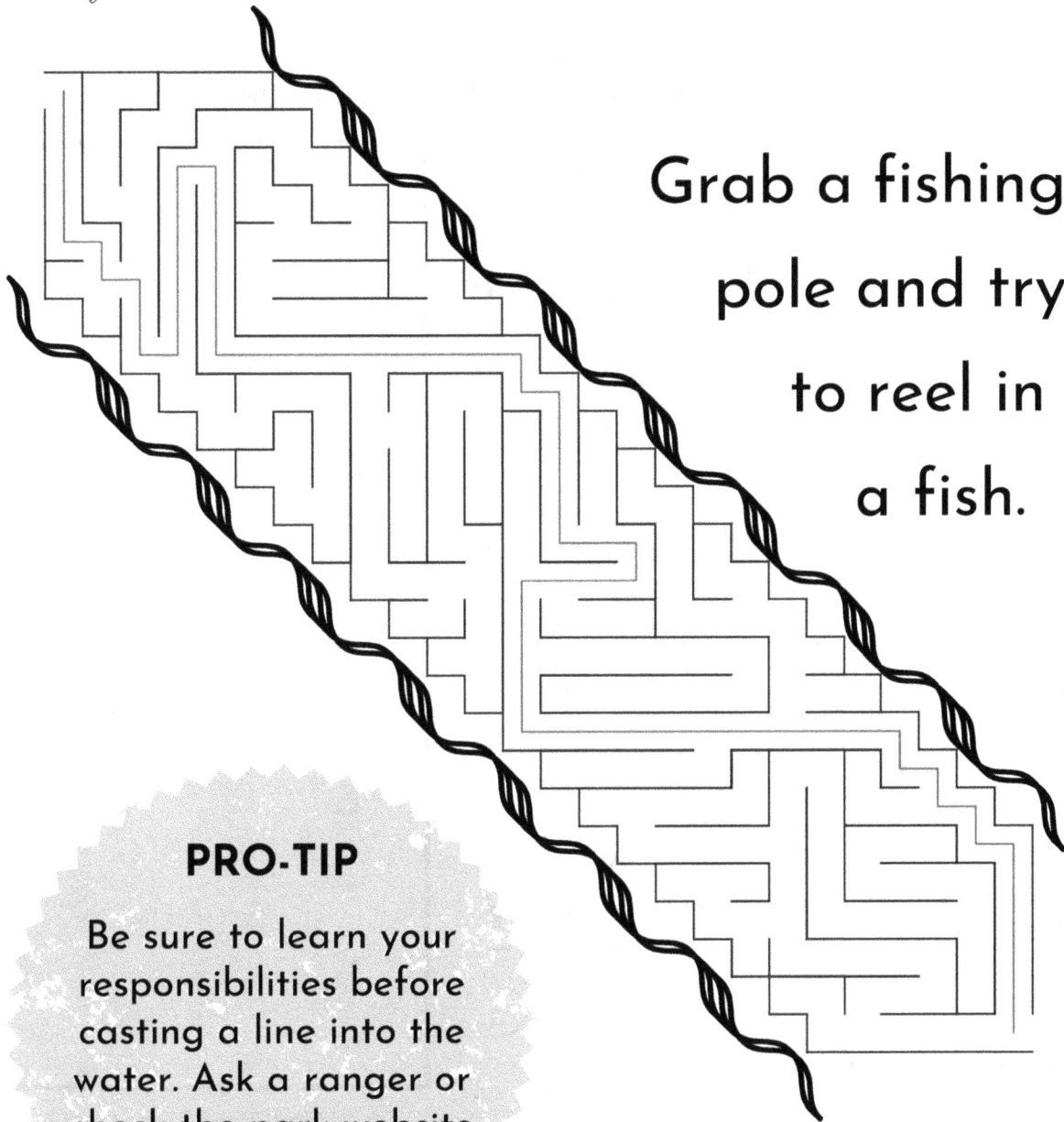

Grab a fishing pole and try to reel in a fish.

PRO-TIP

Be sure to learn your responsibilities before casting a line into the water. Ask a ranger or check the park website before you go.

Decoding Using American Sign Language

American Sign Language, also called ASL for short, is a language that many Deaf people or people who are hard of hearing use to communicate. People use ASL to communicate with their hands. Did you know people from all over the country and world travel to national parks? You may hear people speaking other languages. You might also see people using ASL. Use the American Manual Alphabet chart to decode some national parks facts.

This was the first national park to be established:

Y E L L O W S T O N E

This is the biggest national park in the US:

W R A N G E L L -

S T . E L I A S

This is the most visited national park:

G R E A T S M O K Y

M O U N T A I N S

Aa	Bb	Cc	Dd	Ee
Ff	Gg		Hh	Ii
Jj	Kk	Ll	Mm	Nn
Oo	Pp	Qq		Rr
Ss	Tt	Uu		Vv
Ww	Xx	Yy	Zz	

Hint: Pay close attention to the position of the thumb!

Try it! Using the chart, try to make the letters of the alphabet with your hand. What is the hardest letter to make? Can you spell out your name? Show a friend or family member and have them watch you spell out the name of the national park you are in.

Go Horseback Riding in the Cathedral Valley District

Help find the horse's lost shoe!

start here →

DID YOU KNOW?

Horseback riding is a popular activity in Capitol Reef National Park. There are many trails that you can take horses for day or overnight trips.

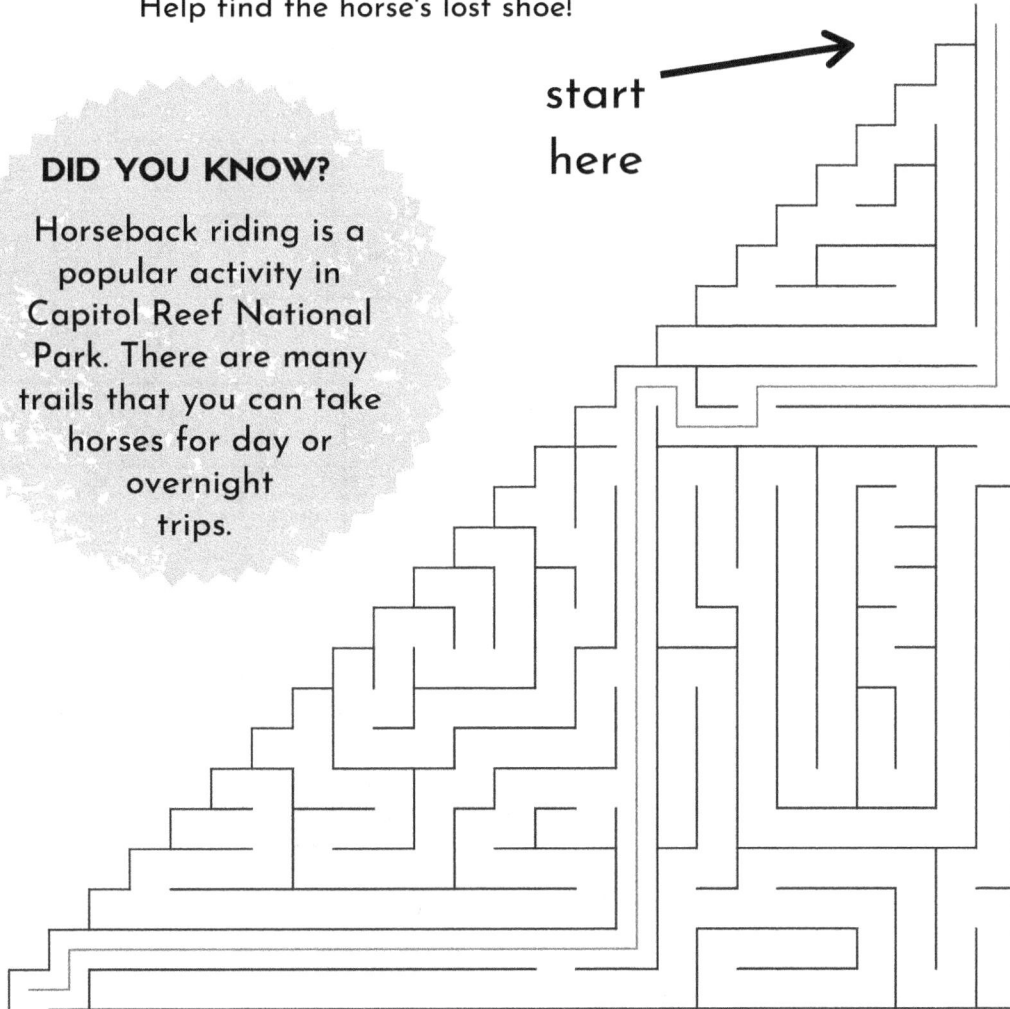

Let's Go Camping
Word Search

1. tent
2. camp stove
3. sleeping bag
4. bug spray
5. sunscreen
6. map
7. flashlight
8. pillow
9. lantern
10. ice
11. snacks
12. smores
13. water
14. first aid kit
15. chair
16. cards
17. books
18. games
19. trail
20. hat

```
D P P I L L O W D B T E A C I
E O A D P R E A A M B R C A N
P W C A M P S T O V E I H X G
R A H S G E L E B E E D A P S
E L B U G S P R A Y N G I E A
S I A H G C I C N N M E R C N
C W N L A F I R S K O O B F K
M T A E M I L E L H M R W L J
T A P R E A O R E S L B A A B
S M P A S R R T E N T L U S C
C E A I I R C G P E I U J H A
S S N A C K S S I M O K I L R
I J R S F O I S N J R A Q I D
C Y E T L E V E G U O R V G S
E W T A K C A B B S S O H H M
X J N F I R S T A I D K I T T
U A A E S S E N G E T P V A B
C J L I A R T D N A M A H A S
```

68

Fish at Capitol Reef

Unscramble these common fish names that live in the park.

1.
SUCKER

2.
OTRTU

3.
CADE

4.
SPINLUC

5.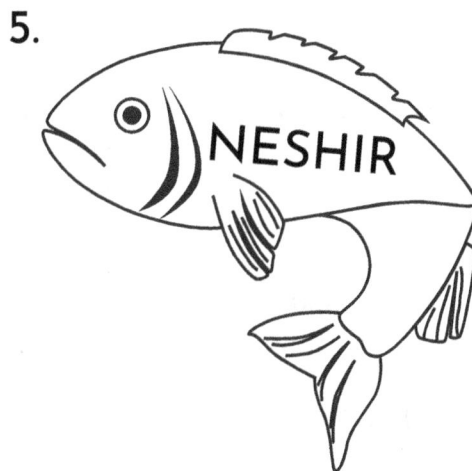
NESHIR

1. __SUCKER__
2. __TROUT__
3. __DACE__
4. __SCULPIN__
5. __SHINER__

Word Bank

dace
sunfish
trout
minnow
sculpin
shiner
whitefish
sucker

Answers: Other National Parks

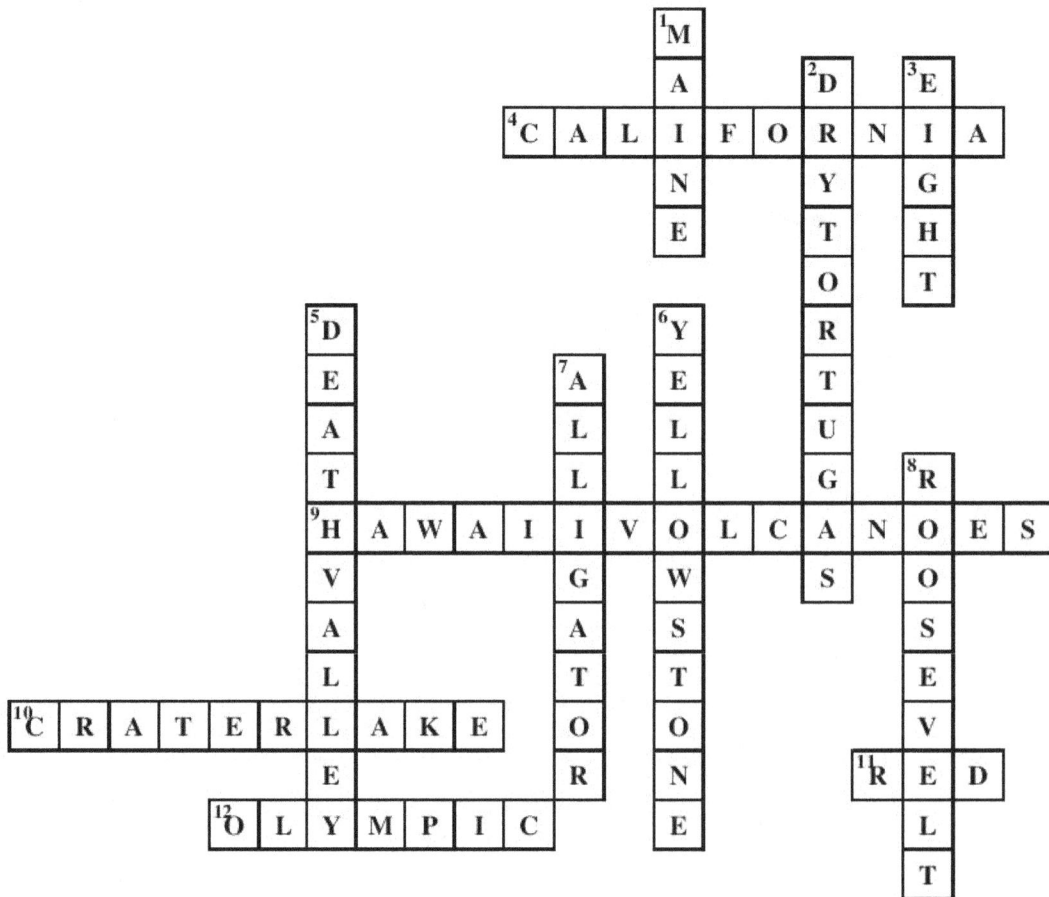

```
                              ¹M
                               A              ²D        ³E
              ⁴C  A  L  I  F  O  R  N  I  A
                               N            Y         G
                               E            T         H
                                            O         T
      ⁵D                          ⁶Y        R
       E                 ⁷A        E         T
       A                  L        L         U
       T                  L        L         G            ⁸R
      ⁹H  A  W  A  I  I  V  O  L  C  A  N  O  E  S
       V                  G        W         S          O
       A                  A        S                    S
       L                  T        T                    E
  ¹⁰C  R  A  T  E  R  L  A  K  E   O                    V
       E                  O        O              ¹¹R  E  D
      ¹²O  L  Y  M  P  I  C        N                    L
                                   E                    T
```

Down

1. State where Acadia National Park is located
2. This National Park has the Spanish word for turtle in it
3. Number of National Parks in Alaska
5. This National Park has some of the hottest temperatures in the world
6. This National Park is the only one in Idaho
7. This toothsome creature can be famously found in Everglades National Park
8. Only president with a national park named for them

Across

4. This state has the most National Parks
9. This park has some of the newest land in the US, caused by a volcanic eruption
10. This park has the deepest lake in the United States
11. This color shows up in the name of a National Park in California
12. This National Park deserves a gold medal

Answers: Where National Park Will You Go Next?

1. Zion
2. Big Bend
3. Glacier
4. Olympic
5. Sequoia
6. Bryce
7. Mesa Verde
8. Biscayne
9. Wind Cave
10. Great Basin
11. Katmai
12. Yellowstone
13. Voyageurs
14. Arches
15. Badlands
16. Denali
17. Glacier Bay
18. Hot Springs

```
F  M  M  E  S  A  V  E  R  D  E  B  N  E  Y
E  A  B  I  G  B  E  N  D  E  S  A  S  E  M
Y  L  I  C  A  L  O  Y  N  E  E  D  L  T  G
D  M  G  A  S  S  A  U  C  N  R  L  U  E  R
C  E  L  I  I  T  S  C  R  E  O  A  A  K  E
S  N  A  W  Y  E  E  O  I  W  T  N  A  C  A
G  I  C  H  A  A  Q  C  S  E  M  D  N  S  T
N  O  I  Z  P  R  U  T  I  M  R  S  N  E  B
I  W  E  L  M  P  O  N  B  W  E  B  K  H  A
R  J  R  F  D  N  I  F  L  I  H  B  U  C  S
P  A  B  E  E  S  A  N  E  S  O  P  W  R  I
S  J  A  E  N  Y  A  C  S  I  B  A  U  A  N
T  C  Y  I  A  D  O  H  H  Y  M  E  A  L  R
O  T  A  T  L  M  L  E  S  E  G  R  W  R  J
H  S  T  O  I  K  A  T  M  A  I  R  O  P  B
I  C  H  U  R  C  O  L  Y  M  P  I  C  O  U
O  Y  G  T  S  D  E  O  S  B  R  Y  C  E  T
W  I  N  D  C  A  V  E  I  N  R  O  H  E  M
```

71

LITTLE BISON

Press

Little Bison Press is an independent children's book publisher based in the Pacific Northwest. We promote exploration, conservation, and adventure through our books. Established in 2021, our passion for outside spaces and travel inspired the creation of Little Bison Press.

We seek to publish books that support children in learning about and caring for the natural places in our world.

To learn more, visit:
LittleBisonPress.com

Want more free games and activities? Visit our website!